THE LION
ENCYCLOPEDIA OF
The Bible

For Lynne,
James, Elizabeth and Leo

P.G.A.

THE LION
ENCYCLOPEDIA OF
The Bible

PETER ATKINSON

LION

Text copyright © 2009 Peter Atkinson
Illustrations copyright © 2009 Peter Dennis
(unless otherwise stated opposite)
This edition copyright © 2009 Lion Hudson

A Lion Children's Book
an imprint of
Lion Hudson plc
Wilkinson House, Jordan Hill Road,
Oxford OX2 8DR, England
www.lionhudson.com
ISBN 978 0 7459 6010 4

First edition 2009
10 9 8 7 6 5 4 3 2 1 0

A catalogue record for this book is available
from the British Library

Typeset in 12/15 Latin 725 BT
Printed and bound in China

Acknowledgments

Design by Emma DeBanks.

Lion Hudson wish to thank Melissa Jackson for her help and advice.

Text Acknowledgments

Bible extracts, unless otherwise stated, are taken or adapted from the *Good
News Bible*, published by The Bible Societies/HarperCollins Publishers Ltd,
UK © American Bible Society 1966, 1971, 1976, 1992.

Selected Bible extracts on pages 10, 14, 15, 21, 37, 39, 43, 89, 97, 106, 108,
112 and 113 are taken from the *Holy Bible, New International Version*, copyright
© 1973, 1978, 1984 International Bible Society. Used by permission of
Zondervan and Hodder & Stoughton Limited. All rights reserved. The 'NIV'
and 'New International Version' trademarks are registered in the United
States Patent and Trademark Office by International Bible Society. Use of
either trademark requires the permission of International Bible Society. UK
trademark number 1448790.

The Lord's Prayer (on page 96) from *Common Worship: Services and Prayers for
the Church of England* (Church House Publishing, 2000) is copyright © The
English Language Liturgical Consultation, 1988 and used with permission.

Picture Acknowledgments

t=top, b=bottom, c=centre, l=left, r=right

Alamy: pp. 98b/© The London Art Archive; 106/© Stock Italia.

David Alexander: pp. 46b, 50l, 55t, 57t, 63c, 80.

The Art Archive: pp. 8/Bibliothèque Municipale Moulins/Gianni Dagli Orti; 10/
British Library; 11b/Fine Art Museum Bilbao/Alfredo Dagli Orti; 12b and 25tr/
Musée du Louvre Paris/Gianni Dagli Orti; 24cl/Bibliothèque Musée du Louvre/
Gianni Dagli Orti; 18c, 26tl and 86b/Gianni Dagli Orti; 30t/British Museum/
Alfredo Dagli Orti; 44/Médiathèque François Mitterand Poitiers/Gianni Dagli
Orti; 49/Anagni Cathedral Italy/Alfredo Dagli Orti; 60/Bodleian Library Oxford,
Bodley 352 folio 13r/The Bodleian Library; 69b/Stei am Rein Switzerland; 70/
National Gallery London/Eileen Tweedy; 77t/Staatliche Glypothek Munich/
Alfredo Dagli Orti; 85/Sta Maria del Carmine Florence/Alfredo Dagli Orti; 88tl/
Archaeological Museum Châtillon-sur-Seine/Gianni Dagli Orti; 92bl, 92br, 93bl
and 93br/Bibliothèque Municipale Abbeville/Gianni Dagli Orti; 103t/National
Museum of Sculpture Valladolid/Alfredo Dagli Orti; 109tr/Alfredo Dagli Orti;
110t/Museo del Prado Madrid; 111c/San Francesco Assisi/Alfredo Dagli Orti;
113/San Apollinare Nuovo Ravenna/Alfredo Dagli Orti.

Corbis: p. 86t/© Araldo de Luca.

The Dean and Chapter of Chichester: p. 38cl.

Kirsten Etheridge: pp. 91, 104t.

Getty Images: pp. 6b/China Photos; 16/Tommaso Masaccio/The Bridgeman Art
Library; 19c/De Agostini Picture Library; 21b/David Silverman; 22/William Blake/
The Bridgeman Art Library; 28tl/Ralph Notaro; 56bl/Jane Sweeney/Lonely Planet
Images; 61/John Roddam Spencer Stanhope/The Bridgeman Art Library; 64/Jack
Guez/AFP; 65t/Persian School/The Bridgeman Art Library; 73b/Bushnell/Soifer/
Stone; 78b/M.Bertinetti/De Agostini Picture Library; 81tr/Gary Cralle/Stone; 82bl/
Roman/The Bridgeman Art Library; 84b/Master of the Female Half Lengths/The
Bridgeman Art Library; 90b/Stephen Studd/Stone; 95/Alistair Duncan/Dorling
Kindersley; 116–117/Pietro Perugino/The Bridgeman Art Library; 118–119/DEA/
W. Buss (De Agostini Picture Library); 104b/French School/The Bridgeman Art
Library.

Lion Hudson: pp. 11t, 82cl and 83t/David Townsend; 33t; 62tl; 102; graphics on
pp. 65b, 92tl.

Rex Nicholls: p. 38 (all instruments).

The Photolibrary Group: pp. 6t and 9b/The Print Collector/Imagestate; 13t/
Miro Vintoniv/Index Stock Imagery; 15b/Lee C Coombs/Phototake Science; 14/
IFA-Bilderteam GMBH/IFA Animals; 15t/Kathie Atkinson/Oxford Scientific
(OSF); 17/Juniors Bildarchiv; 18–19/Bowman/F1 Online; 27/Robert Harding/
Robert Harding Travel; 30b/Botanica; 39br/Jochen Schlenker/Robert Harding
Travel; 45/Karl Ammann/Picture Press; 59br/N Jaubert; 81c/Hanan Isachar/
Jon Arnold Travel; 87/De Agostini Editore; 89/Anders Tukler/Nordic Photos;
108/Ivan Vdovin/Jon Arnold Travel.

Lois Rock: p. 98t.

Adrian Walmsley: pp. 48l, 97c, 111b, 115r.

Richard Watts: maps pp. 6–7, 13b, 21t, 37t, 47cl, 55b, 57b, 72, 76, 78t, 90t,
100, 105, 110b.

Z. Radovan/www.BibleLandPictures.com: pp. 9t, 12t, 23b, 33t, 36, 41tr, 47cr,
46t, 56cr, 79, 103b, 109bl, 117t.

Picture research below courtesy of Zooid Pictures Limited.

Mary Evans Picture Library: p. 53.

United Nations Photo Library: p. 66/Andrea Brizzi.

World Council of Churches: p. 69t.

Alamy: p. 118tl/Jeff Greenberg.

Still Pictures: p. 119tr/Sarah Filbey/Christian Aid.

Contents

1 What is the Bible?

The Bible is the holy book of Christians. In the Bible, Christians believe they discover the truth about God and find help to live their lives well.

The word 'Bible' sounds like the name of a single book, but it comes from *biblia*, which is the Greek and Latin word for 'books' in the plural. The Bible is in two parts, the Old Testament and the New Testament, each of which is made up of many books by different writers. (Another name for the Bible is the Holy Scriptures, which means the 'holy writings'.)

The Old Testament tells the story of the people of Israel (later called the Jews) up to the time of the Roman empire. The New Testament tells the story of a Jewish teacher called Jesus and his followers – the first Christians – who lived during the first century.

People of other religions also read the Bible, or parts of it. What Christians call the Old Testament is also holy to the Jews. The stories of the Bible are important for Muslims as well, though they have their own holy book called the Qur'an. *The Lion Encyclopedia of the Bible* will look mainly at the Bible as the holy book of Christians.

A page from the *Book of Kells*, an illuminated manuscript edition of the four Gospels, made in Ireland in about 800 CE. Before printing, every Bible had to be copied out by hand.

A modern paperback edition of the Bible in Chinese script. The Bible has been printed more times than any other book.

The stories of the Bible are set in what we now call the eastern Mediterranean and the Middle East – from modern Italy to modern Iran.

The books of the Bible are ancient. They were written and collected over a long period of time and they need to be studied in the same way as other ancient books. We have to know about the languages and customs of those times. We have to know the archaeology and history of the period. We need the help of experts who have studied all these subjects.

There is much in the Bible that is hard to understand. Some people find the way God is spoken about in some parts of the Bible difficult to accept. But not every part of the Bible has equal importance for Christians. For Christians, Jesus Christ is the main character, and it is the story of Jesus that helps to make sense of the rest of the Bible.

Christians belong to communities called churches. (The word 'church' is also often used to describe the buildings Christians worship in.) Different churches have their own way of reading and understanding the Bible, often using different translations. But in every church the Bible is read aloud during worship. In earlier times, before printing made it possible for Christians to have their own copies of the Bible at home, they could only know what was in the Bible by hearing it read aloud in church. And even today, with the Bible in print and online, Christians believe that it is still important to read the Bible and to try to understand it *together*.

Books about the Bible can also make it easier to read. That is the aim of *The Lion Encyclopedia of the Bible*.

Books, chapters and verses

Almost all the books of the Bible are divided into chapters, and those chapters are divided again into verses. These divisions help us to find a single sentence in the Bible very easily, but it is important to remember that the original writers did not divide up their books like this. The chapter divisions were put into the Latin version of the Bible in the middle ages. Stephen Langton, who was a famous Bible scholar, and the archbishop of Canterbury from 1207 to 1228, is thought to have made the chapter divisions. Verse divisions were first used in the sixteenth century.

In *The Lion Encyclopedia of the Bible*, Genesis 1:1 means the book of Genesis, chapter 1, verse 1. Genesis 2–6 means the book of Genesis, chapter 2 to chapter 6. Genesis 32:22 – 33:17 means the book of Genesis, chapter 32, verse 22, to chapter 33, verse 17.

Some books have the same name. For example, Paul wrote two letters to the Corinthians. So 1 Corinthians means his first letter, and 2 Corinthians means his second letter. 1 Kings means the first book of the Kings, and 2 Kings means the second book of the Kings.

The Bible quotations in this encyclopedia are mostly from the *Good News Bible*, with some from the *Holy Bible, New International Version*.

Jerusalem

2 Powerful Stories

Look it Up

David and Goliath:
1 Samuel 17

Daniel in the lions' den:
Daniel 6

Jonah, swallowed by the fish, in a twelfth-century Bible. No doubt the artist enjoyed painting this picture as much as the reader enjoyed reading the story – without worrying too much about what really happened.

Scribes

Some parts of the Bible were at first passed on by word of mouth, and only later written down, often by the people the Old Testament calls 'scribes' (or 'secretaries'). These were rather like today's civil servants. The people New Testament calls scribes (or 'teachers of the Law') taught religion to the people, and like the Pharisees were often opposed to Jesus (but not always – see Mark 12:28–34).

The Bible is a collection of many different kinds of books – law, history, prophecy (or special messages from God), songs and wise sayings. But above all the Bible is a collection of stories. From the story of creation in the book of Genesis at the beginning, to the story of the final victory of God in the book of Revelation at the end, the Bible tells powerful stories. Even when they are funny stories (and some are – including some of the stories Jesus told), they still make a serious point. They are stories that can change the way people live.

Did it really happen?

A question that is often asked about a story is: 'Did it really happen?' This question is asked about the stories of the Bible. The answer is that some did and some didn't. Many of the stories in the Bible are real history. We know that from the findings of archaeology and the historical records of other ancient peoples. But not everything in the Bible is real history. Some of it is just meant to be a story, like the stories that Jesus himself told. The stories Jesus told were not supposed to have 'really happened'. For example, Jesus told a story about a man who was attacked by robbers on a desert road and left for dead. Two people from the man's own country came past, but didn't stop to help. Then came someone who was from a different country. People from the two countries usually hated each other. But he was the one who stopped to help the injured man. Jesus told the story to show that people from different countries can still be our 'neighbour'. The story has a serious point, and one that we can follow, even though the story didn't 'really happen'.

Giving hope for the future

People have always told stories about the past to help them understand what is happening to them in the present, and to give them hope for the future. The Jewish people, who have often been made to suffer by others, have drawn strength and courage from their

8

Archaeology can confirm many Bible stories. The 'Taylor Prism', discovered in Sennacherib's palace in Nineveh and now in the British Museum in London, refers to his campaign against King Hezekiah of Judah.

stories. For example, in the terrible days of the Second World War, when millions of Jews were imprisoned and killed, they told each other the stories of David against Goliath, and Daniel in the lions' den. These were stories from the past that helped them understand their present experience. They were like Daniel facing the lions or David facing Goliath. The stories also gave them hope for the future. They helped them to hold fast to their faith that God would save them again, just as he had in the times of David and Daniel.

Christians have also suffered persecution, in the time of the Roman empire and at later periods. A book like the Revelation of John has been a source of hope and encouragement to Christians at such times.

Stories as a source of wisdom

The stories of the Bible are not only for hard times. They have a wisdom that has helped many people live their lives well during times of peace too. The proverbs (or wise sayings) of the Old Testament and the stories that Jesus told have this wisdom. So do the stories of those who tried to live well – Abraham, Joseph, Ruth, Job, Peter and Paul. The law books of the Old Testament have helped many countries decide their own laws, although not all the laws in the Old Testament are right for today's world. There is a wisdom for every mood and occasion in the Psalms, which has made them among the best-loved songs in the world. Indeed, it can be said that there is a wisdom for every mood and occasion in the Bible as a whole, which has made it one of the most-read books in the world.

Parables

Jesus told stories called 'parables', which comes from a Greek word that means a 'likeness' or a 'comparison'. For example, he told his followers:

The kingdom of heaven is like this. A man is looking for fine pearls, and when he finds one that is unusually fine, he goes and sells everything he has, and buys that pearl.

Matthew 13:45–46

Jesus says that God's kingdom is so precious and so important that people should make it the most valuable thing in their lives: just like a trader in jewels who sells everything they have in order to buy one fine pearl.

The story of Daniel in the lions' den has been a favourite with generations of Jews and Christians. This is from a fifth-century Roman mosaic.

3 Passing it On: Copying, Printing and Translating

Look it Up

Jerome's translation:
Chapter 32

Counting the years [BCE/CE]:
Chapter 39

Different translations

Compare Mark 10:13–16 in the Good News Bible and the New International Version:

Good News Bible:

Some people brought children to Jesus for him to place his hands on them, but the disciples scolded the people. When Jesus noticed this, he was angry and said to his disciples, 'Let the children come to me, and do not stop them, because the Kingdom of God belongs to such as these. I assure you that whoever does not receive the Kingdom of God like a child will never enter it.' Then he took the children in his arms, placed his hands on each of them, and blessed them.

New International Version:

People were bringing little children to Jesus to have him touch them, but the disciples rebuked them. When Jesus saw this, he was indignant. He said to them, 'Let the little children come to me, and do not hinder them, for the kingdom of God belongs to such as these. I tell you the truth, anyone who will not receive the kingdom of God like a little child will never enter it.' And he took the children in his arms, put his hands on them and blessed them.

Before printing, Bibles were copied out by hand. An illustration of St Dunstan, archbishop of Canterbury in the tenth century, writing at his desk.

Before printing was invented, every book had to be copied out by hand. A book copied by hand is called a 'manuscript'. There was no printing in the lands of the Bible during the period in which the books of the Bible were being written. (Printing was not invented in Europe until the fifteenth century CE, although the Chinese had used a form of printing centuries before that).

Copying was slow, laborious and expensive. Ordinary people could not have their own books. From the time of the New Testament onwards, each Jewish or Christian community would have its own set of sacred books, all in manuscript. Rulers and other rich people might collect books, and there were some large libraries in the ancient world. The books of ancient writers, such as the classical authors of Greece and Rome, were carefully looked after, but not always carefully enough. A fire could destroy a library, and priceless books were sometimes lost for ever. The Christian monasteries housed some of the most important libraries in medieval times.

Sometimes the owners of a book did not realize how rare it was. They wanted the paper for another book, and paper was expensive. So the book was scraped clean, and the paper used again.

Copying a book was not easy. It was hard work and sometimes boring. So mistakes quite easily crept in. Sometimes the person making the copy would add comments of their own – especially if they disagreed with what they were copying!

Many printed Bibles have footnotes that explain how a word might have different meanings. Almost every page of the Bible has some word or phrase that is in one manuscript but not in another. It is the task of 'textual' scholars to work out which is likely to be the best version. But even if every page of the Bible has one or two doubtful words or phrases in it, that shows how much of the text of the Bible is clear and agreed.

Of course, once printing was invented, everything changed. Mistakes became more unusual (though printers can make mistakes too!). Books could be mass-produced, and so became cheaper. For the first time, ordinary people could own their own Bible. The 'family Bible', shared by the whole household and passed down the generations, was popular in many countries.

Long before then, of course, the Bible had been translated out of its original languages. The Jews of Alexandria in Egypt translated the Hebrew Bible into Greek, and much later, the Christian scholar Jerome translated both the Old and New Testaments into Latin (the language of the Romans). The Bible was mainly used in Latin in the Middle Ages in western Europe, though some parts of the Bible were translated into the local languages as well. For example, the first complete English translation was made by John Wycliffe in the fourteenth century. Since then, the Bible has been translated into more than 2,000 languages.

No translation can ever exactly capture the meaning of the original. That is why two translations of the same book can look so different from each other. Each translator must work out a way of putting the meaning of the original across. The new language may not have one word that corresponds with a word in the original; or it may have too many words, and the translator must make a choice. The making of translations involves the work of many experts who need to know the ancient languages well.

The Codex Sinaiticus: one of the most important Greek manuscripts of the Bible, made in Egypt in the fourth century AD and now in the British Museum in London.

The scroll and the codex

The books of the Old Testament were written on scrolls, and so were the writings of many other ancient cultures. There are many references to scrolls in the Old and New Testaments. But by the second century CE, Christians were pioneering a new way of making books. Instead of rolling one sheet up, and starting another roll, they began to write on one sheet after another, and all the sheets were then sewn together down one side. It is what we think of as an ordinary book (in Latin it called a 'codex') – but the Christians made it popular! We don't quite know why the Christians adopted the codex so enthusiastically. Of course the 'codex' is a very convenient way of making a book, which is why books have continued to be made in this way. But in the second century, it was one of the things that marked Christians out from people of other religions.

St Jerome, the Bible scholar who translated the Bible into Latin in the fourth century. From a sixteenth-century Flemish painting.

4 What is the Old Testament?

The language of the Old Testament

Nearly all the books of the Old Testament were written in Hebrew, the language of the people of Israel. (Parts of the book of Daniel and what is called the Apocrypha were written in Aramaic and some other parts of the Apocrypha in Greek.)

Aramaic is a language closely related to Hebrew, and was widely used in the lands conquered by the Assyrians. Aramaic was the language Jesus was probably brought up to speak, and the Gospels give us a few words of Aramaic spoken by him (for example, *Abba*, meaning 'Father').

The books of the Old Testament are arranged according to what looks like a simple plan. This begins with the creation of the world in Genesis 1. Later in Genesis, God chooses Abraham to become the ancestor of a new people. These people came to be called 'Israel' or 'the Israelites', the 'Hebrews', or, even later, the 'Jews'. From then on the Old Testament spells out the history of this people, with its customs and laws, as well as the words of its great teachers the 'prophets', and the writings of others called the 'wise'.

The plan looks straightforward, but the books of the Bible weren't written in such a simple way. Stories were passed on by word of mouth, from one generation to the next, before anyone wrote them down. Gradually these stories were collected into books. Some of the books of the Old Testament are made up of what began as several books, later added together. Later still, all the holy books of Israel were brought into one collection, and the order decided on. The book of Genesis now comes first in the Old Testament, but that does not mean that it was the first book to be written. One of the oldest parts of the Old Testament is the Song of Deborah in the book of Judges, which is the seventh book of the Old Testament.

We don't know the names of all the people who wrote the books of the Old Testament. Different writings from different times were sometimes collected under the name of one writer. For instance, the first five books of the Old Testament are called the 'books of Moses', although they show signs of having been gradually put together over a long period of time. The fifth 'book of Moses', Deuteronomy, describes the death of Moses, so Moses certainly didn't write that bit! The writing and rewriting and collecting of the books that in the end made up the Old Testament was going on for many hundreds of years, and was only finished after the capture of Jerusalem by the Romans in 70 CE.

Above: a fragment, from about 100 BCE, of the book of Isaiah in Hebrew, from the Dead Sea Scrolls discovered at Qumran.

The Old Testament was written mainly in Hebrew, unlike the New Testament, which was written in Greek – like this fragment of manuscript from the Gospel of Luke.

The Hebrew Bible is read aloud in synagogues all over the world every sabbath.

The Old Testament is made up of many different *sorts* of books. There are books of law – the laws and customs of the people of Israel. There are books of history – the records of the people of Israel, the stories they told of their early days, and the words spoken by the prophets as their history unfolded. And the books we call the 'wisdom' books – the writings of the 'wise' – are proverbs, and songs and reflections on life. They all make up the one great story of the people of Israel, which is the story of the Old Testament.

The land of the Old Testament has been known by many names. This is a map of the kingdoms of Israel and Judah after the time of King Solomon, with their neighbouring kingdoms.

Proverbs

Wise children make their fathers proud of them; foolish ones bring their mothers grief.

Proverbs 10:1

The land of the Old Testament

A large part of the story of the Old Testament concerns a *land*. The people of Israel believed that God promised this land to Abraham, so it is sometimes called 'the **Promised Land**'. Abraham's descendants first settled there, then went to Egypt, then returned and settled there again. In this part of the Old Testament, the land is often called **Canaan**, and the original people of the land Canaanites. The people of Israel called the land **Israel**, one of the names of Jacob. When the kingdom was divided in two, the two kingdoms were called **Israel and Judah**.

Another name for the land is **Palestine**. This was a name used by the Greeks and Romans, after another of the peoples who lived there, the Philistines.

Today, 'Israel' is the name of the Jewish state founded in 1948, and those who live there are now called 'Israelis'. 'Palestine' is the name of the territories that form the homeland of the Arab peoples of the land. The boundaries between the two are disputed by the Israeli and Palestinian authorities.

5 In the Beginning: Genesis

Look it Up

The story of God making the world in six days:
Genesis 1:1–31; 2:1–3

The story of God making the Garden of Eden:
Genesis 2:4–25

'It was very good'

Both Genesis 1 and Genesis 2 say that God made the world good. Genesis 1:31 says: 'God saw all that he had made, and it was very good.' This is an important part of the faith of both Jews and Christians. There have been some religions which have said the opposite. They have said that the physical world is bad. But Judaism and Christianity teach that the physical world and the life of the human body are God's good gifts.

The first words of the first book of the Bible are 'In the beginning…' The name 'Genesis' is a Greek word which means 'beginning'. The book of Genesis begins with two stories of how the universe began.

Genesis 1 tells how God made the universe in six days and rested on the seventh day. In this story, God simply gives the command, and different parts of the world come into existence. God starts with light, and then he makes the stars, the earth, the animals and finally human beings. God looks at what he has made and sees that it is 'very good'.

In Genesis 2, the story of creation is told in quite a different way. Here God begins by making a man called Adam (the name in Hebrew simply means 'man'), and then planting out a garden for him in a land called Eden. God forms the animals to be Adam's companions, and then forms a woman whom Adam calls Eve, the 'mother of all the living.' They live together in the Garden of Eden and eat the fruit from the trees. These include the tree of life, but God tells them that there is one tree from which they must not eat. This is the tree that gives knowledge of good and evil. God wants to shield them from knowing what evil is.

These two stories are quite different from each other. Many scholars think that the whole of Genesis has been woven together from different stories. However the book was put together, the different stories complement each other. In their different ways these two stories of how the world began have the same message: that the human race has a special place in God's design. Genesis 1 says that humans are made to be like God, and God gives to them the care of the world. Genesis 2 shows the natural world as home for the human race, and Adam gives names to the animals. But neither story says that humans can do what they like with the world. They are there to look after it on God's behalf.

In the beginning, when God created the universe, the earth was formless and desolate. The raging ocean that covered everything was engulfed in total darkness, and the Spirit of God was moving over the water.

Genesis 1:1–2

Human beings have always been awed by the majesty of the natural world. Those who believe in God see in the natural world a reflection of his majesty.

Fossils indicate the immense age of the earth.

Creation and evolution

Genesis 1 and Genesis 2 do not tell the story of the beginning of the universe in the same way that most scientists do. Most scientists (many of whom are Christians) think that the universe evolved over an immense period of time. Many other Christians agree with them. These Christians believe that God caused the universe to come into existence (and this is what they mean by 'creation'); that the universe has evolved over millions of years; and that the stories in Genesis are a poetic way of putting this into words. Other Christians believe that the universe was made by God in six days (and this what *they* mean by 'creation') and that the theory of evolution is wrong.

The Milky Way. The first chapter of Genesis tells how God made 'light' which was then resolved into stars, suns and moons…

6 The Story of the Fall

Look it Up

The story of the fall:
Genesis 3

Who is the serpent?

The serpent who tempts Eve to eat from the forbidden tree is simply one of the animals in the Garden of Eden. The story doesn't say that the serpent was evil, only that he was 'cunning' – he was good at asking crafty and unexpected questions. The Old Testament never says that the serpent is the devil, or Satan, or an enemy of God. It is not until we get to the book of Revelation in the New Testament that the devil is called 'the dragon, that ancient serpent'. In that book, the devil is defeated by the archangel Michael. He falls from heaven and comes down to earth in great anger. Christians later put the story of the Garden of Eden and the story of Michael and the dragon together, so that it looked as though the serpent in the Garden of Eden was the devil in disguise.

Chapter 3 of the book of Genesis tells how Adam and Eve were persuaded by the cunning serpent to eat the fruit from the tree of the knowledge of good and evil.

So they disobeyed God. They spoiled their life in the Garden of Eden and now they had to leave it. Adam would have to work hard to grow food for them to eat, and Eve would find it painful to give birth to children. They were now ashamed of being naked in front of God and they sewed fig leaves together to make clothes for themselves. This is the story of the 'fall' – how men and women 'fell from grace' and lost the sense of being close to God. But although they had to leave the garden, God still cared for them. Later in the story, God gave them animal skins to wear.

The faces of Adam and Eve in this painting by the fifteenth-century artist Masaccio show their grief at leaving the Garden of Eden.

The story of Adam and Eve says something that many people have found true about their own lives. For many people, life is full of sadness and disappointment. Work is often hard and boring. Childbirth is painful and can be dangerous. The message of the story of the Garden of Eden is that God means life to be better than it is. It has made many people long to find that closeness to God that Adam and Eve enjoyed in the Garden of Eden.

One of the famous teachers in the early centuries of Christianity was a man called Augustine (354–430). He wrote a prayer that captures the sense of longing for that closeness to God: 'You have made us for yourself, and our hearts are restless until they find their rest in you.'

The story of Genesis is a reminder that the natural world is for men and women to care for, not to exploit.

The naming of the animals

Genesis 2 describes how God brought all the animals and birds to Adam for him to give them names. In the ancient world, naming something was often thought to be a way of having power over it. So when God brings the animals to Adam to be named, it is a way of saying that Adam is given control of the natural world. But it is not a way of saying that human beings can do what they like with animals and birds. When the prophet Isaiah pictured the world as God meant it to be, he thought of animals and humans living peaceably together.

7 A World of Wickedness

Look it Up

The story of Noah's ark:
Genesis 6–10

The story of the Tower of Babel:
Genesis 11:1–9

The story of Noah's ark has been a favourite with artists down the centuries. An early seventeenth-century stained-glass window in the church of St Etienne du Mont, Paris.

The story of the human race, as the book of Genesis tells it, becomes more violent. Adam and Eve have two sons, called Cain and Abel. Cain murders Abel in a fit of jealousy. As the human race grows, so do violence and anger and all that the Bible calls 'sin'.

The story of Noah's ark

Genesis 6 tells how God decided to wipe out the human race and start again. He chose one good man called Noah, with his family, and a male and a female of all the different animals. A great flood destroyed all life on earth, but at God's bidding, Noah built a ship (or 'ark') for his family and for his animals. For 40 days they rode out the flood, and then the waters subsided. The story tells how the ark came to rest on the mountains of Ararat, and Noah and his family began life all over again.

At the end of the story, God promises never again to destroy all living beings with a flood. Noah sees the rainbow, so often seen when the sun comes out after rain, as God's promise that the great flood is gone for good.

The story of Noah raises the question whether God really punishes people with floods or other disasters.

Mount Ararat, on the borders of modern Turkey, Armenia and Iran, is the setting for the story of Noah's ark.

The story of Noah was written at a time when many people thought that everything powerful, whether good or bad, simply came from God. If there was a terrible flood, then God must have made it happen; and if God made it happen, then it must have been because people deserved it. Some people still think like that today, but the overall message of the Bible gives a different idea of God. In the book of Job, Job learns that terrible things happen to good people as well as bad; and in the Gospels, Jesus says that things like disasters and diseases are not God's punishments on wicked people.

The story of the Tower of Babel

A later story in the book of Genesis tells how people decided to build a great tower into the sky. It was a show of strength and pride. But God muddled up their language so that people could no longer understand what they were saying to each other. They were scattered in confusion and ended up living in different parts of the world with different languages. Even today, the difference of language is one of the biggest barriers to people understanding each other and living together peacefully.

Other stories of the flood

Many ancient cultures told stories of a great flood. The Greeks told how the god Zeus punished the wickedness of human beings by flooding the world. But King Deucalion escaped by building an ark that came to rest on Mount Parnassus.

In a Babylonian story called the Epic of Gilgamesh, a man called Utnapishtim also escapes the flood in an ark.

There is no archaeological evidence of a great flood that covered the whole earth wiping out all but a few human beings. But there is evidence of severe regional floods in low-lying areas such as Mesopotamia (modern Iraq). It is likely that it was the memory of such floods that gave rise to the story of the great flood.

Temples such as this – called ziggurats – were part of the culture of ancient Sumeria, Babylon and Assyria. Perhaps it was such a building that suggested the story of the Tower of Babel.

8 Journey into the Unknown: Abraham

Look it Up

The story of Abraham:
Genesis 11:10 – 25:11

John the Baptist:
Chapter 40

The children of Abraham

In the time of Jesus, the people of Israel were proud to be the descendants of Abraham. But John the Baptist, Jesus and Jesus' followers changed what being 'descended from Abraham' meant. John the Baptist warned the people of Israel that God still expected them to live good and upright lives, and not just to rely on being 'descendants of Abraham' (Luke 3:7–9). In John's Gospel, Jesus says, 'Your father Abraham rejoiced that he was to see the time of my coming; he saw it and was glad' (John 8:56). In Galatians 4:21 – 5:1, Paul points out that Abraham had two sons – not just Isaac, from whom the people of Israel were descended, but Ishmael as well. So being 'descended from Abraham', Paul argued, meant more than just being a blood relation: it meant having the faith in God that Abraham had.

Chapters 1 to 11 of the book of Genesis tell stories about the beginning of the world and the early adventures and experiences of human beings. They are stories whose roots lie lost in the mists of time. But from Genesis chapter 12, a new story begins. God chooses one man, whose name at first was Abram, and who lived in what is now Iraq, to begin a journey into a strange country. This was the land where one day his descendants, so God told him, would form a great nation – the people of Israel (or the Hebrews or Jews). The land which God promised them is that which today is Israel and Palestine. What follows in the Old Testament is the story of this people and the land they believed that God had given them.

Abram's family lived in Ur, later moving to Haran. It was there that God told him to go to find his new land. Abram's wife Sarai had no children, so it was hard to see how God's promise that he would be the ancestor of a great nation could come true. As was the custom of the time, Abram had a child by Sarai's slave girl, Hagar. This child was called Ishmael. But God spoke to Abram again and told him that Sarai would still bear the son from whom the chosen people would be descended. God changed Abram's name to Abraham, and Sarai's name to Sarah. In her old age, Sarah gave birth to a son, Isaac. Abraham is the first of the three 'patriarchs', the ancestors of the people of Israel.

The story of Abraham has two shocking moments. Genesis 22 tells the story of how God told Abraham to kill Isaac as a sacrifice. It was meant as a test of Abraham's faith, for how could God's promise of a great nation of descendants come true if his son were dead? The story tells how Abraham was on the point of killing Isaac when God told him to stop.

The story of Abraham and Sarah tells how, in their old age, God gave them a baby, from whom God's chosen people would be descended.

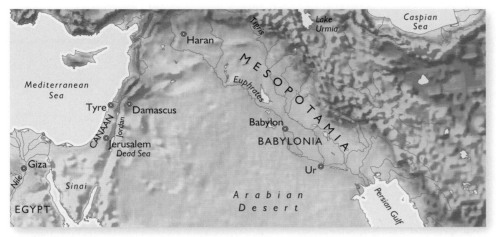

Abraham travelled from Ur to Canaan by way of Haran.

In another story (in Genesis 18), God plans to destroy the city of Sodom, which is full of wicked people. But Abraham's nephew Lot and his family also live there, and Abraham begs God to spare the city for the sake of the innocent people living in it. Abraham bravely argues with God, and says to him, 'Will not the Judge of all the earth do right?' God allows Lot's family to escape, but he does not spare the city.

These are stories that show God as terrible and full of revenge. But they also show people like Abraham beginning to question such a way of thinking about God. 'Will not the judge of all the earth do right?' is a hugely important question for anyone to ask about God. In these stories, the message is beginning to emerge that the God who made the world is also merciful and just.

The call of Abraham

The Lord said to Abram, 'Leave your country, your relatives, and your father's home, and go to a land that I am going to show you. I will give you many descendants, and they will become a great nation. I will bless you and make your name famous, so that you will be a blessing.

I will bless those who bless you,
But I will curse those who curse you.
And through you I will bless all the nations.

Genesis 12:1–3

Genesis 19 tells how Lot's wife was turned into salt as Lot and his family escaped from Sodom. The city of Sodom was near the Dead Sea, a salt sea that leaves deposits of salt round its shores.

Changing names

Often in the Bible, people are given new names at important new stages of their lives. God changes Abram to Abraham, and Sarai to Sarah. In Hebrew, Abram means 'exalted father'; Abraham means 'father of a multitude'. Both Sarai and Sarah mean 'princess', but the change of the name showed that she too was making a new beginning in her life.

In the Gospels, Jesus gives Simon the new name of Peter, when he becomes his follower. Also, the author of the Acts of the Apostles calls Saul by his Jewish name to begin with, but when he starts his great work preaching the Christian message, he calls him Paul.

Circumcision

In Genesis 17:9–14, God tells Abraham that all his male descendants must be circumcised when they are eight days old. Circumcision is the removal of the foreskin, which may also be done for medical reasons. Luke records the circumcision of the baby Jesus (Luke 2:21). Paul insisted that Gentile (non-Jewish) people who became Christians did not have to be circumcised – they did not have to become Jews before they could be Christians.

9 A Promised Land: Isaac and Jacob

Look it Up

The story of Isaac:
Genesis 24 – 28:9; 35:27–29

The story of Jacob:
Genesis 25:19 – 37:2

Jacob at Bethel

Jacob woke up and said, 'The Lord is here! He is in this place, and I didn't know it!' He was afraid and said, 'What a terrifying place this is! It must be the house of God; it must be the gate that opens into heaven.'

Genesis 28:16–17

The second and third of the great 'patriarchs' were Abraham's son Isaac, and Isaac's son Jacob.

The book of Genesis recounts how Abraham, after he had settled in the land of Canaan, told his servant to go back to the city of Haran to find a wife for Isaac from among Abraham's family. The servant returned with Rebecca, the daughter of Abraham's nephew. Isaac loved Rebecca, and she bore him two sons, Esau, and his younger twin brother, Jacob. There was rivalry between them from the beginning, and when Isaac was very old and unable to see, Jacob tricked him into giving him the blessing that was reserved only for the first-born son. Jacob had to escape from Esau, although, after many adventures, they were reconciled.

A well-known story of Jacob tells how one night he reached a certain place and fell asleep. He dreamed that he saw a ladder going from earth to heaven with the angels of God going up and down on it. God spoke to Jacob and made him the same promise that he had made to his grandfather Abraham: that the land would belong to his descendants, and that they would be a great nation. 'The Lord is here!' said Jacob to himself when he woke up. 'He is in this place, and I didn't know it! … It must be the house of God; it must be the gate that opens into heaven'. By 'the Lord', Jacob meant God. He named the place Bethel, which means 'the house of God' in Hebrew, and later it became an important city.

In another story, Jacob wrestled all night long with a stranger who turned out to be an angel of God, or even God himself. Jacob demanded to know the stranger's name, but he would not tell him. He wounded Jacob, but at the end of the struggle he blessed him and gave him a new name, Israel. The picture of a human being wrestling with God is surprising; but like the story of Abraham arguing with God, it suggests that there is nothing easy or comfortable about believing in God. It can be a struggle; it can be painful. The message of the story of Jacob is that in the end it brings blessing.

Jacob's dream, from a painting by the early nineteenth-century English artist, William Blake.

Jacob wanted to marry Rachel, the younger daughter of his uncle Laban, for whom he worked. Laban made him work for seven years before he agreed to the marriage, and then he tricked Jacob into first marrying his elder daughter, Leah. Jacob the trickster was himself tricked for once. Leah and Rachel, and their two maids, gave Jacob a total of twelve sons. Their descendants formed the twelve tribes of the people of Israel. Ten were named after sons of Jacob, and two after Ephraim and Manasseh, the two sons of Joseph. The tribe of Levi, who were the priests of Israel and had no land of their own, were counted as an extra tribe.

The brothers Jacob and Esau, reconciled after years of being enemies.

The site of Bethel today.

Bethel

The city of Bethel was excavated by archaeologists in the early part of the twentieth century. They found evidence of a thriving city of the Middle Bronze Age (2000–1500 BCE), which was around the period of the patriarchs, Abraham, Isaac and Jacob.

10 Journey to Egypt: Joseph

Look it Up

The story of Joseph:
Genesis 37–50

An Egyptian harvest scene from the tomb of Mennah in Thebes, dating from perhaps 1390 BCE.

The later chapters of Genesis are taken up with one of the longest stories in the Old Testament, the story of Joseph. We don't know who wrote the story, but it has all the drama and suspense of a good novel. It tells of a young man living by his wits and rising to the highest position in the kingdom of Egypt.

Joseph was the youngest but one of the twelve sons of Jacob. He and his younger brother, Benjamin, were the only two of Jacob's sons born to him by Jacob's much-loved wife Rachel. Joseph was Jacob's favourite and his older brothers hated him. One day they sold him to slave-traders on their way to Egypt and told Jacob that he had been killed by a wild animal.

This wall painting from the tomb of Khnum-hotep III at Beni Hasan (about 1890 BCE) shows Asian travellers arriving in Egypt wearing 'coats of many colours'.

Joseph and the coat of many colours

The book of Genesis says that Jacob gave Joseph a fine coat. The Hebrew is quite hard to translate, and the traditional translation is 'a coat of many colours'. Modern translations usually say it was a 'robe with full sleeves'. Either way, it was clearly a fine garment for someone not expected to work hard in the fields like the rest of Jacob's sons.

In Egypt, Joseph was made the slave of the captain of the palace guard. The captain's wife wanted Joseph to go to bed with her, and when he refused she said that he had tried to force her. The captain had him thrown into prison. He was let out when he was the only person who could explain the king's dreams. They meant that a terrible famine was approaching, and Joseph was put in charge of storing up grain so that the country would not starve.

The famine reached the land of Canaan and Jacob sent his elder sons to buy grain in Egypt. They found themselves in front of Joseph without knowing who he was. He made them bring their youngest brother, Benjamin, with them on their next visit. This time, Joseph played a trick on them – his silver cup was discovered in Benjamin's sack of grain as if he had stolen it. One of the brothers, Judah, offered his life instead of Benjamin's. Joseph was very moved and finally told them who he was. Joseph and his brothers were reconciled, and the whole family moved down to Egypt where Joseph gave them land for their sheep, and where he cared for Jacob in his old age. So the family of Jacob (who was also called Israel) came to live in Egypt, away from the land God had promised to Abraham.

Look it Up

The story of Moses and the escape from Egypt:
Exodus 1–15

Slaves making bricks. A wall painting from a tomb in the Valley of the Nobles at Qurna from about 1400 BCE.

The cities of Egypt

According to Exodus, the Hebrew slaves built Pithom and Rameses. Historians don't know where Pithom was, but Rameses was probably at the 'Nile delta' (where the River Nile reaches the Mediterranean sea). A palace of Pharaoh Ramesses II and other great houses have been discovered there. Ramesses II (sometimes called 'the Great') is thought to have been the pharaoh at the time of the Exodus. He ruled Egypt from 1279 to about 1212 BCE and he is famous for a great victory against the Hittites at Kadesh on the River Orontes in Syria in about 1286 BCE.

The second book of the Old Testament is called Exodus, a Latin word which means 'escape'. It tells how the people of Israel (or the Hebrews, as they are often called in this part of the story) escaped from Egypt, where they had become slaves.

For a time, all had gone well in Egypt with Jacob's sons and their families. But as time passed, the Egyptians came to hate these foreigners living among them. After Joseph had died, a later pharaoh (king) made the Hebrews into slaves and forced them to build great cities at Pithom and Rameses.

The Egyptians still feared the Hebrews, and the pharaoh next ordered all the newborn Hebrew boys to be killed. One family had a baby boy whom they hid in a basket made of reeds beside the River Nile. He was discovered by Pharaoh's daughter and taken to her palace. He was named Moses and brought up as a prince. But his own mother was allowed to look after him, and from her Moses learned that his true people were the Hebrews.

One day, when he was grown up, Moses saw an Egyptian kill one of the Hebrew slaves. Moses killed the Egyptian and hid his body. But what he had done became known. Moses went into hiding in the Sinai desert and became a shepherd. Once, he was on Mount Sinai (also called Mount Horeb) when he saw a bush on fire, and, as he stared at it, God spoke to him. God told him to go back to Egypt to lead the people of Israel out of slavery to the Promised Land. Moses was terrified at the idea, but God said that his brother Aaron would be there to help him.

God also told Moses his own name. His name, God said, was 'I AM'.

Moses and Aaron went to Pharaoh and asked for the people of Israel to be set free and allowed to leave Egypt. Not surprisingly, Pharaoh said no. God began to bring plagues to the land – frogs, gnats, hail, and the River Nile turning to blood. The last plague was that the firstborn sons of the Egyptians died, just as Pharaoh had killed the sons of the Hebrews.

Moses was sure that Pharaoh would now let them go, and told the people to eat a hurried meal in readiness for their journey. The plague of death struck the people of Egypt, but 'passed over' the people of Israel. They always remembered that hurried 'passover' meal, and repeated it as a festival each year.

They set out from Egypt, but at once Pharaoh changed his mind and sent an army of chariots to bring them back. The people of Israel were able to cross the Red Sea (or the 'Sea of Reeds') where the water allowed them a way through, but the Egyptian chariots became stuck and many of the soldiers were drowned.

The people of Israel, with Moses at their head, now set out on the long journey through the desert, back to the land of Canaan.

This detail of Tutankhamun hunting from a painted box found in his tomb in the Valley of the Kings evokes the Egyptian army sent to pursue the escaping Hebrews.

The feast of the Passover

The Passover (Pesach) is one of the three great festivals of the Old Testament. The other two are the feast of Weeks (Shavnot) and the feast of Shelters (Sukkot – see chapter 29). Every spring, each household re-enacted the hurried supper that Moses ordered the people of Israel to have before they escaped from Egypt. The Passover meal consists of lamb and bread which had not been leavened, or made to rise properly. The bread was unleavened because there was no time for it to leaven. Jewish people still celebrate the Passover every year. The 'Last Supper' that Jesus had with his disciples (see chapter 54) was their Passover meal.

The name of God

God told Moses that his name was 'I AM'. In Hebrew this name has just four letters: YHWH, usually pronounced 'Yahweh'. In English, this name is also sometimes given as 'Jehovah'. The people of Israel felt the name was too holy to say aloud, so instead they said 'the Lord'. In English translations of the Bible, YHWH is sometimes given as Jehovah or Yahweh, but more often as 'the LORD', spelled in capitals.

Look it Up

The journey to the land of Canaan:
Exodus 16–19; 24; 32–40

This chest, made to be carried on poles and discovered in the tomb of Tutankhamun, shows what the ark of the covenant might have looked like.

The ark of the covenant

'Ark' is an English word which is used both for the vessel or boat which Noah built (see chapter 7) and also for the sacred box which the people carried through the desert and later placed in the Temple at Jerusalem. Deuteronomy says that the two tablets of stone on which the Ten Commandments were written were placed in the ark. For the people of Israel, wherever the ark was, there was God. When the Babylonians captured Jerusalem in 586 BCE, the ark was either captured or destroyed. Later, there were many legends about the ark being hidden until God at last brought all his people home from exile (see 2 Maccabees 2:4–8).

Having escaped from Egypt, the Hebrews' troubles were not over. They became hungry and thirsty in the desert. The book of Exodus tells how God looked after them. Food (called 'manna') fell from heaven. When they were thirsty, God told Moses to strike the rock with his staff, and water flowed out of it. At last they crossed the Sinai peninsula and came to Mount Sinai, where God had spoken to Moses from the burning bush.

Moses climbed the mountain, and there God gave him the laws by which the people of Israel were to live. Much of the book of Exodus is taken up with these laws. The most famous of them are the 'Ten Commandments', which were inscribed on two tablets of stone.

This cutaway picture shows what the ark, standing inside the tabernacle, may have looked like. The tents of the people of Israel are gathered around it.

God also gave Moses instructions to make a tent (or 'tabernacle') for the people to carry with them on their journey. Inside the tent there was to be no image of God, as in the temples of other peoples, but instead there was to be a box known as the 'ark of the covenant'. The two tablets of stone, on which the Ten Commandments were written, were to be kept in it.

But when Moses came down the mountain, the people had already forgotten God and were worshipping the golden image of a calf, and in his anger Moses broke the tablets of stone. The people were sorry for what they had done, and came back to worship God. Eventually the tabernacle and the ark were made to God's instructions, and new tablets of stone were written. The presence of God filled the tabernacle, which was covered by a cloud. When the people of Israel could see the cloud, they knew that God was present. When the cloud moved on, the people continued their journey, following God to the land of Canaan.

There are more of the laws of the people of Israel in the books of Leviticus, Numbers and Deuteronomy. These reflect different periods in the history of Israel and only were gradually collected together as the 'Law of Moses'.

The Ten Commandments

1. *Worship no god but me.*

2. *Do not make for yourselves images of anything in heaven or on earth or in the water under the earth.*

3. *Do not use my name for evil purposes.*

4. *Observe the sabbath and keep it holy.*

5. *Respect your father and your mother.*

6. *Do not commit murder.*

7. *Do not commit adultery.*

8. *Do not steal.*

9. *Do not accuse anyone falsely.*

10. *Do not desire another man's house… or anything else that he owns.*

From Exodus 20:3–17

Harsh punishments

Many of the punishments for breaking the laws of the Old Testament are harsh – for example, Deuteronomy says that a woman who commits adultery is to be put to death. Many ancient and primitive cultures had harsh laws, and the laws of other ancient lands were often more severe than the Old Testament. All the same, the Bible is often criticized for having such harsh punishments in it.

Christians are not bound by all the laws of Moses. For example, it was explained in chapter 8 that non-Jewish men who became Christians were not expected to be circumcised, although that is part of the Law of Moses.

Not all the laws of Moses were harsh. There is much that is compassionate and good, and much that people of all religions and cultures would agree with. Laws such as 'you shall not murder' and 'you shall not steal' are part of what is now called international law.

13 Return to Canaan: Joshua and the Judges

The famous judge Gideon led an attack against the Midianites. This Assyrian relief from about 645 BCE shows Midianite soldiers riding camels.

From Joshua's final speech

'*If you are not willing to serve him, decide today whom you will serve, the gods your ancestors worshipped in Mesopotamia or the gods of the Amorites, in whose land you are now living. As for my family and me, we will serve the Lord.*'

Joshua 24:15

Moses himself never reached the land of Canaan. After 40 years of travelling, as told in the book of Numbers, the people of Israel arrived at the River Jordan, on the borders of Canaan. But on the way, there had been a moment when even Moses was disobedient to God, and God told him that he would never enter the land himself. From the top of a mountain, Moses could see the land to which he had led the people. He died there and was buried, 'but,' says Deuteronomy, 'to this day nobody knows the exact place of his burial.'

Moses' second-in-command, a man called Joshua, now led the people. The book of Joshua tells how they crossed the Jordan and began to take possession of the land. The land of Canaan was not an empty one. People lived there already; it was their home. One of the best-known stories of the book of Joshua is the capture of the city of Jericho. The story goes that the people of Israel marched round the walls of Jericho for seven days, carrying the ark of the covenant. On the seventh day, the priests all blew trumpets, the people shouted – and the walls of Jericho collapsed. The city was left without defences, and the Israelites rushed in to capture it. Apart from a woman called Rahab and her family, who had helped some Israelite spies, all the people of Jericho were put to death. The Israelites captured some cities, and in others they persuaded the people to join them.

So the people of Israel settled back into the land of Canaan. Before they had kings, their rulers were known as 'judges', and the book of Judges tells the stories of those days. The three most famous judges were Deborah, Gideon and Samson.

A view of Jericho and the Jordan valley today.

Deborah was a strong leader. During her time as judge, the army of Israel won a great victory against an army of Canaanites. The Canaanite commander, Sisera, fled from the battlefield, and was killed by another brave woman, Jael, who drove a tent peg through his head while he lay exhausted.

Gideon is known for leading a daring attack against the Midianites, and defeating them with a small force of chosen soldiers and the use of clever shock-tactics.

Samson is legendary for his amazing strength, which he used to defeat the Philistines. But Samson was in love with Delilah, who was being paid by the Philistines, and she persuaded him to tell her the secret of his strength. His parents had dedicated him to God when he was born, and as a sign of that they had promised never to cut his hair. That was the secret of his strength. So one day, while he slept, Delilah had his long hair cut off. He lost his strength, and the Philistines captured him, blinded him and then put him on show while they feasted. But with one last surge of strength, he broke the pillars of the building, and it collapsed on his enemies.

Is this what God is like?

In this part of the Old Testament, God commands the people of Israel not only to put the local people of Canaan out of their homes, but to put them to death as well. It is a terrifying picture of a God who could command such massacres, an even worse picture than the story of the flood (see chapter 7).

The idea of God changed and developed as time went on. From being thought of as the bloodthirsty god of just their own tribe, the people of Israel came to think of him as the Lord of the whole earth, and eventually as a God for all people. This change of thinking is reflected, for example, in the stories of Abraham, Job, Isaiah and Jonah.

In Christian teaching, the changing idea of God comes to its full development in the life of Jesus. The development of the idea of God is one of the most important themes of the Bible.

Archaeologists are not agreed whether a violent invasion of the land of Canaan ever took place. The early people of Israel may have been less murderous than they seem to be in their own stories!

The Canaanite army of chariots was defeated by the Israelites at the River Kishon (Judges 4).

14 A Girl Seeking Asylum: Ruth

Look it Up

The story of Ruth:
Ruth 1–4

The law of gleaning:
Leviticus 19:9–10

King David:
Chapter 16

Ruth's promise to Naomi

But Ruth answered, 'Don't ask me to leave you! Let me go with you. Wherever you go, I will go; wherever you live, I will live. Your people will be my people, and your God will be my God. Wherever you die, I will die, and that is where I will be buried. May the Lord's worst punishment come upon me if I let anything but death separate me from you!'

Ruth 1:16–17

The story of Ruth is a quiet contrast to the blood and battles of the book of Judges. Many Bible stories are about men, and usually the men of Israel. Here is a story about two women, one of them a foreigner. Some Bible stories tell of miracles, amazing events directly made to happen by God. Here is a story about people who believe in God, but God doesn't keep getting into the story. They work out their own lives in difficult times, make their decisions as best they can, and hope to find happiness. The surprise at the end of the story is that Ruth's child becomes the grandfather of the boy who in turn grew up to be the most important king in Israel's history, King David. So Israel's greatest king was descended from a penniless girl seeking asylum in a foreign land.

The background of the story is that an Israelite man went to live in the neighbouring land of Moab to find work and food when there was a famine in Israel. He took his wife Naomi and their two sons. The sons married two Moabite women called Orpah and Ruth. In the end, both the father and sons died, and the three women were left alone. Naomi decided to go home to the land of Israel and look for her relatives. Ruth decided to go with her.

Ruth is very loyal to her mother-in-law, Naomi. 'Wherever you go, I will go,' she says; 'wherever you live, I will live. Your people will be my people and your God will be my God.' They travel to Naomi's home town, Bethlehem. The harvest is just beginning. Ruth looks for work in the fields. There is a law in the book of Leviticus that says that when fields were harvested, poor people were allowed to 'glean': that is, to pick up bits of corn that the reapers who gathered the crops left behind them. This was a way for both poor people and foreigners to find food.

Bethlehem means 'house of bread'; the word for 'house' can also be seen in the place name Bethel, which means 'house of God'.

Moab

Wars between Israel and Moab are mentioned elsewhere in the Old Testament, so the story of King David's descent from a Moabite girl is all the more surprising. The kingdom of Moab lay to the east of the Dead Sea (in modern Jordan). Its god was Chemosh, mentioned several times in the Old Testament. In 1868 a stele (stone tablet with an inscription) was discovered. The inscription is by King Mesha of Moab (see 2 Kings 3) thanking Chemosh for victory over his enemies.

The baby of Bethlehem

The story of Ruth has a special meaning for Christians. Jesus belonged to the family of King David (and so of Ruth as well). Ruth's son, and later King David as well, were born in Bethlehem; and so was Jesus. The book of Ruth tells how the people of Bethlehem welcomed Ruth and celebrated the birth of her baby. Luke's Gospel tells how the shepherds of Bethlehem went to greet Mary and *her* newborn son, Jesus.

Ruth works in the fields of a rich man named Boaz. He notices the young woman and tells his men to leave plenty of corn for her to glean. Ruth tells Naomi about her day's work and the name of the farmer, and Naomi realizes that he is a member of her family. Naomi encourages Ruth to join the farm workers when they all sleep together in the barn at night and, at the right time, remind Boaz that he is a relative and should take care of her. Boaz decides that he would like to marry Ruth. There is a difficulty when it turns out that Naomi has a closer relative than Boaz, and, according to the custom of the time, Boaz has to ask him first whether he wants to marry Ruth. But the other relative says no, and soon Boaz and Ruth are married. Ruth has a baby boy, and Naomi helps to look after him. The child grows up in Bethlehem, as does his son Jesse, as does *his* son David.

Much later in the Bible, a descendant of Ruth called Joseph will take his wife Mary to Bethlehem for her baby to be born there, and those working in the fields of Bethlehem will rejoice again at the birth of a child.

The inscription on the Mesha Stele (also called the Moabite Stone), found in 1868, is by King Mesha of Moab. Ruth came from Moab.

15 Choosing a King: Samuel and Saul

What sort of king?

The book of Deuteronomy, set in the time of Moses, describes how the people of Israel might one day ask for a king. If they have a king, says Deuteronomy, then he must rule according to the Law. The king is not to be 'above' the Law, doing as he likes. The idea that the king is bound to the Law is surprising for the time: it took other cultures a very long time to catch up with the Old Testament.

The last of the great judges was Samuel. In his time, the ark of the covenant was kept at a place called Shiloh. Samuel was brought up there, having been dedicated to God as a baby, as a young boy called by God to serve him. Samuel combined the tasks of judge, priest and prophet, but after years of being ruled by the judges the people wanted a warrior-king, like other nations.

The beginning of the first book of Samuel tells how Samuel warned the people against having a king, but eventually God told Samuel to choose a strong man called Saul. Samuel anointed Saul with oil, the sign of being made king. God commanded Saul to go into battle against a neighbouring tribe called the Amalekites and destroy them all, but Saul spared the life of the king of the Amalekites as well as the best of his flocks and herds. The story tells how God was angry with Saul for his disobedience, and ordered Samuel to choose another king. Samuel picked out David, the youngest son of Jesse, who came from Bethlehem. He anointed David as a sign that one day he would be king after Saul.

The calling of Samuel

1 Samuel 1 tells how Samuel was dedicated to God by his parents as a baby and brought up in Shiloh, where the ark of the covenant was kept. He was the assistant to the priest Eli, who looked after the ark. Eli was very old, and had two sons who did not follow God. One night, the young boy Samuel heard God calling him by name. Thinking it must be Eli, he went to see what he wanted. Twice Eli told him to lie down again, but the third time Eli realized that God was calling him. So he told Samuel to reply, 'Speak, Lord, your servant is listening.' When God called him again, Samuel said, 'Speak; your servant is listening,' and God told him that Eli's sons would never serve him. As Samuel grew up, everyone realized that he was someone God spoke to, and they trusted him to be their judge. Old Eli died, and his two sons were killed in battle.

As the first king of Israel, Saul had no capital city. 1 Samuel 11 mentions Saul's 'house' at Gibeah in the tribal territory of Benjamin, north of Jerusalem. Archeological excavations have revealed several layers of buildings on the site, including a fortress with towers and walls from about the time of Saul. Saul continued to live among his fellow-Benjaminites, and his family would have continued to support themselves by farming.

Anointed kings

The kings of the Old Testament were anointed with oil: that was the sign of being a king, though priests were also anointed. The Hebrew for 'anointed' is *mashiah*, which gives the English word 'messiah'. When in the time of Jesus people were hoping for the Messiah, it was an 'anointed king' they expected. The Greek word for 'anointed' is *christos*, which gives us our word 'christ'. So 'Jesus Christ' means Jesus the Messiah, or Jesus the anointed king.

16 The Great King: David

Look it Up

The story of David:
1 Samuel 16–31; 2 Samuel 1:1 – 24;
1 Kings 1:1 – 2:12

David at his worst...

The worst thing David did was to arrange for one of his soldiers, a man called Uriah, to be killed, after David had fallen in love with his wife, Bathsheba. David had seen Bathsheba from his rooftop while she was bathing. She became pregnant with his child, and David gave secret orders for Uriah to be put in the most dangerous part of a battle. The other soldiers were told to fall back, leaving Uriah alone and defenceless. Once Uriah was dead, David married Bathsheba. Their child died, but Bathsheba later gave David another son, Solomon.

A brave man called Nathan came to David and told him a story. The story was about a rich man who had all he needed, and a poor man who had one small lamb. Yet the rich man took the lamb away from the poor man. David was very angry, and threatened to punish the rich man. But Nathan said to him, 'You are the man.' This brought home to David the great wrong he had done.

Goliath was a Philistine soldier. This figure of a Philistine is from the temple of Ramesses III, pharaoh 1187–1156 BCE.

David, who is considered to be the greatest of Israel's kings and the most popular hero of the Old Testament, reigned about a thousand years before Jesus lived. Little is known about him from outside the Bible, although in 1993 archaeologists did find an inscription in Galilee which mentions both the 'house of David' and the 'king of Israel', dating from a century after his time. What we read about David in the Bible is recounted by an unknown scribe who was one of the most brilliant writers of ancient times.

The story which this anonymous scribe tells is full of adventure. The most famous story told about David is how he fought with the giant Goliath. Goliath was a Philistine soldier and stood nine feet (nearly three metres) tall. None of the Israelite soldiers would fight him, but David, who was only a boy, killed him with a sling and a stone. David became a hero to the people of Israel, and a close and devoted friend to the king's son, Jonathan. King Saul was bitterly jealous, and tried to kill him, but David escaped into the desert with a company of followers. Saul and Jonathan were both killed in battle, and David's words of grief over them is one of the most poetic passages in the Bible.

David then became king, and ruled his people firmly but not always well. He fell in love with the wife of one his commanders and arranged for him to be killed in battle so that he could marry her. One of his sons, Absalom, rebelled against him, was defeated in battle and then was killed when he was trapped in a tree by his long hair. David grieved for Absalom, as he had done for Saul, even though he had defeated them both. David captured the city of Jerusalem from a tribe called the Jebusites and made it his capital. He defeated the Philistines, and made peace for his people.

The writer tells the story of David from his boyhood in Bethlehem to his old age in Jerusalem. He describes David's achievements without making them into miracles, and his faults without excusing him. This makes his story all the more fascinating.

In the troubled centuries that followed, people looked back to his reign as a golden age. They clung to God's promise that the prophet Nathan spoke to David (2 Samuel 7:16): 'You will always have descendants, and I will make your kingdom last for ever.' Later the prophet Isaiah said, 'A shoot will come up from the stump of Jesse; from his roots a Branch will bear fruit.' That was the promise that one day there would be a new king of Israel, and the kingdom of David would be restored. Such a person, like David, would be God's anointed one – the Messiah.

David dances before the ark as it is carried into Jerusalem, his new capital city.

David is remembered as having enlarged the borders of Israel and making Jerusalem its capital. The kingdom never reached such a size again.

David at his best...

One of David's most generous actions was to do with the son of his dear friend Jonathan, the son of King Saul. After Saul and Jonathan had been killed in battle, one of Jonathan's sons was proclaimed king in Israel, and there was further fighting between his followers and the army of David. Jonathan's son was defeated and murdered by David's men. But Jonathan had another son, Mephibosheth, who was only five years old, and who had been so injured while his family were escaping from David's men that he was permanently disabled. As the surviving grandson of King Saul, he might easily have been proclaimed king, and David might have thought it best to have him killed as well. But he took pity on him, for the sake of his father Jonathan. David brought him to live in his own palace, and took care of him for the rest of his life.

17 The Songs of the Kingdom: the Psalms

A window in Chichester Cathedral by Marc Chagall (1978) illustrating Psalm 150, a psalm of praise. It shows all the musical instruments mentioned in the psalm, as well as the menorah, the seven-branched lampstand.

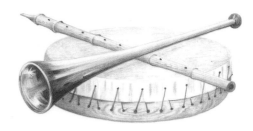

tambourine, flute and trumpet

The book of Psalms contains the worship songs of the Old Testament. The word 'psalm' means a song sung to the harp. Some of the psalms were composed for a group to sing – perhaps hundreds of pilgrims visiting the Temple. Others are more individual. Some are songs of praise; others express sorrow for sin, or are prayers to God in time of trouble. Some are prayers for the king, and perhaps they celebrate a victory in battle. The psalms show delight, hope, anger and despair. The psalm-writers were not afraid to let God know just how they were feeling.

The psalms come from different periods and were written by different people. Some are called 'Psalms of David', while others are said to be by Solomon or other people. It is easy to imagine King David (who had been both a shepherd boy and a harp player) singing the most famous of all the psalms, which begins 'The Lord is my shepherd' (Psalm 23).

In many of the psalms, an idea is expressed in one line, and then the same idea is expressed in the next line using different words.

double trumpet and shofar

lyre

rattle, clappers, harp and cymbals

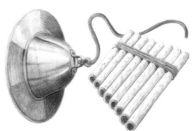

cymbal and pan-pipes

This is an example from Psalm 24:

The world and all that is in it belong to the Lord;
the earth and all who live on it are his.

He built it on the deep waters beneath the earth
and laid its foundations in the ocean depths.

Who has the right to go up the Lord's hill?
Who may enter his holy Temple?

Those who are pure in act and in thought,
who do not worship idols or make false
promises.

The Lord will bless them and save them;
God will declare them innocent.

Such are the people who come to God,
who come into the presence of the God of
Jacob.

This helped to make the psalms easier to remember, for the people who first used them had to learn them by heart. Today, the psalms are still sung in Jewish and in Christian worship, and provide a prayer for every mood and occasion.

David is remembered as both king and musician, 'the composer of beautiful songs for Israel'.

The best-known psalm: Psalm 23

The Lord is my shepherd;
I have everything I need.

He lets me rest in fields of green
grass and leads me to quiet pools of
fresh water.

He gives me new strength.

He guides me in the right paths,
as he has promised.

Even if I go through the deepest
darkness, I will not be afraid, Lord,
for you are with me.

Your shepherd's rod and staff protect
me.

You prepare a banquet for me,
where all my enemies can see me;

you welcome me as an honoured
guest and fill my cup to the brim.

I know that your goodness and love
will be with me all my life; and
your house will be my home as long
as I live.

Sheep graze safely beside quiet pools.

Jesus and the Psalms

Jesus was brought up to know and love the psalms, and often quoted from them. On the cross, he said the opening words of Psalm 22: 'My God, my God, why have you abandoned me?' The early Christians continued to sing the psalms in their worship, many of which spoke to them of Jesus. Psalm 8, for instance, says:

What is man that you are mindful of him,
the son of man that you care for him?

You made him a little lower than the heavenly beings
and crowned him with glory and honour.

This reminded the first Christians of Jesus, often called 'the Son of man'.

18 The Wise King: Solomon

The Temple of Solomon

The Temple of Solomon is described in 1 Kings 6–8. From this we know that it was a rectangular building, about 30 metres long, 15 metres tall and 10 metres wide. At the front was the porch (the *'ulam*) flanked by two bronze pillars. Inside were two rooms. The first was the 'Holy Place' (the *hikhal*) and here stood an altar on which incense was burned morning and evening. The inner room was the 'Holy of Holies' (the *debir*). Here in total darkness was kept the ark of the covenant. The top of the ark, called the mercy-seat, was thought of as the throne of God, flanked by the 'cherubim' (angelic beings).

David was succeeded by his son Solomon. Solomon's mother was Bathsheba, whom David took from her husband after he had him killed in battle. Solomon grew up in a court that was full of plots and conspiracies. He learned to be crafty; he learned to be wise. The first book of Kings tells how Solomon worked wisely to strengthen his kingdom. Solomon encouraged trade agreements with other lands, and he enlarged and beautified the city of Jerusalem. Solomon had many wives, including women from other countries, and later Old Testament writers criticize him for that. Perhaps the greatest thing for which he is remembered was the building of the Temple in Jerusalem as a permanent home for the ark of the covenant.

Above all, Solomon is celebrated for his 'wisdom'. One story that is told of his wisdom concerns two women.

A reconstruction of Solomon's Temple.
1. The sea of bronze
2. The altar
3. The porch
4. The holy place
5. The Holy of Holies
6. The ark of the covenant
7. The cherubim
8. The menorah

Each had a baby, but one baby died in the night, and both mothers wanted the one baby that was left. Solomon ordered the baby to be chopped in two! One woman agreed that that would be fair; at least neither of them would have it. The other woman cried out in anguish and begged the king to give the baby to the first woman rather than kill it. Solomon knew that the second woman was the child's real mother, and gave it back to her.

People came from far and wide to visit his court. 'King Solomon was richer and wiser than any other king,' says the writer of 1 Kings, 'and the whole world wanted to come and listen to the wisdom that God had given him.'

The gold seven-branched lampstand or menorah stood in the Temple as a sign of God's presence.

His most famous visitor was the queen of Sheba. We do not know where the land of Sheba was, but if it is the same as the land of the Sabaeans, also mentioned in the Bible, then it was probably in the southern Arabian peninsula. Because of his reputation for wisdom, Solomon gave his name to several of the 'wisdom' books of the Old Testament and the Apocrypha.

Psalm 122

Psalm 122 is a song of praise to God to be sung by those going to the Temple.

*I was glad when they said to me,
'Let us go to the Lord's house.'*

*And now we are here,
standing inside the gates of Jerusalem!*

*Jerusalem is a city restored
in beautiful order and harmony.*

*This is where the tribes come,
the tribes of Israel,*

*to give thanks to the Lord
according to his command.*

*Here are the kings of Israel
sat to judge their people.*

*Pray for the peace of Jerusalem:
'May those who love you prosper.
May there be peace inside your walls
and safety in your palaces.'*

*For the sake of my relatives and
friends, I say to Jerusalem, 'Peace be
with you!'*

*For the sake of the house of the Lord
our God I pray for your prosperity.*

19 The Sayings of the Wise: the 'Wisdom' Books

Look it Up

A poem in praise of wisdom:
Proverbs 8

A love poem:
Song of Songs 8:5–7

A lament for the hardships of old age:
Ecclesiastes 11:9 – 12:8

Ecclesiastes

Ecclesiastes is a book that says that life is short and sometimes unhappy. It is almost the mirror image of the Song of Songs. Its opening words are: 'Meaningless! Meaningless! … Utterly meaningless! Everything is meaningless.' All the same, it is full of 'wisdom', and ends with the advice: 'Have reverence for God, and obey his commands, because this is all that human beings were created for.'

'Wisdom' is a word that means many things in the Old Testament. It means knowing how to make the most of life. It means managing other people and getting the best out of them. It means the skill of the artist or the craftsman. It means using all the gifts God has given.

In the Old Testament, wisdom comes from God, and knowing God is the way to learn wisdom: 'The way to become wise is to honour the Lord' (Psalm 111:10).

Much of the wisdom of the Old Testament is in the form of **proverbs**. These are short sentences, easily remembered, and passed on from one generation to another. These are some of them: 'Drinking too much makes you loud and foolish. It's stupid to get drunk' (Proverbs 20:1). 'Some friendships do not last, but some friends are more loyal than brothers' (Proverbs 18:24). 'If you spend your time sleeping, you will be poor' (Proverbs 20:13). 'A gossip can never keep a secret. Stay away from people who talk too much' (Proverbs 20:19).

These examples are from the book of Proverbs. Other proverbs, and other writings about wisdom, are in two books of the Apocrypha: 'The Wisdom of Solomon', and 'The Wisdom of Jesus son of Sirach (Ecclesiasticus)' (see chapter 33).

'Work and you will earn a living…'

Wisdom was needed by those who worked for the king. Each royal court had a staff of officials trained in the administration of the kingdom. Much of the 'wisdom' writing in the Old Testament comes from these court officials. For example, Proverbs 25 was 'copied by men at the court of King Hezekiah of Judah'. There are very strong similarities between this kind of writing and that of ancient Egypt.

Stories about the 'wise' were also popular. In Genesis, Joseph is shown as the ideal 'wise man', serving at the royal court, living by his wits, and managing other people. Daniel outwits the Babylonian wise men because he is wiser than they are. 2 Samuel and 1 Kings tell of life at the courts of King David and King Solomon and the officials and soldiers who served them.

'… if you sit around talking, you will be poor' (Proverbs 14:23).

A time for everything

There is a time for everything, and a season for every activity under heaven:
a time to be born and a time to die,
a time to plant and a time to uproot,
a time to kill and a time to heal,
a time to tear down and a time to build,
a time to weep and a time to laugh,
a time to mourn and a time to dance…

Ecclesiastes 3:1–4

'Wisdom' at the court of the pharaoh

The writer of 1 Kings gives as an example of the 'wisdom' of King Solomon that he 'composed 3,000 proverbs and more than a thousand songs. He spoke of trees and plants… he talked about animals, birds, reptiles, and fish.' The making of such lists was typical of the 'wisdom' literature of ancient Egypt. One example is the *Onomasticon of Amenope*, written about 1085 BCE, which lists 610 things that make up the universe, ranging from the sky, water and earth, to the towns of Egypt, types of land, and the parts of an ox!

The Song of Songs

Another book, also said to be by Solomon, is the Song of Songs. It is a love poem. Although God is not mentioned in the book, the fact that it is part of the Bible says something important about God. It says that the love of one person for another, and the delight that they take in each other's bodies, are gifts from the God who made all things good.

20 A Wise Man Faces Up to God: Job

Look it Up

Job's life is ruined:
Job 1–2

Job complains to God:
Job 3, 29–31

God answers Job:
Job 38–41

Job's prosperity is restored:
Job 42

Writing about suffering in the ancient world

The book of Job is not the first book to struggle with the question why innocent people suffer. There are texts from ancient Sumeria in what is now Iraq (3000–2000 BCE), and from Egypt (2000–1800 BCE) that address this question, but perhaps the closest parallel is from Babylon. The *Babylonian Theodicy* (from about 1100 BCE) is a poem in which a man tells his friend about everything that has gone wrong for him, and his friend tries to comfort him. They both wonder why the gods allow such things to happen, but they don't discover any convincing answers.

There is no evidence that the author of the book of Job had read the *Babylonian Theodicy*. Both books have emerged from cultures which addressed important questions through imagined debates between friends.

Many of the proverbs tell us that the wise will be successful and God will reward them. 'It is the Lord's blessing that makes you wealthy.' 'Storms come, and the wicked are blown away, but honest people are always safe' (Proverbs 10:22, 25).

It isn't known who wrote the book of Job, but whoever it was, they challenged this 'wisdom'. They imagined a story in which a good man suffered through no fault of his own.

The man's name was Job. He was the 'richest man in the East'. He worshipped God and 'was careful not to do anything evil' – exactly as a 'wise' person should. God was very proud of Job, and pointed him out to Satan. (The word 'Satan' means 'the accuser'. In this book, he is not the devil, but a heavenly being with a special part to play in the story. He is a prosecutor, who makes 'accusations' about people.) But Satan scoffed and said that Job only worshipped God because Job

had everything he wanted. Job would be a very different person, Satan suggested, if things began to go wrong.

Things do go wrong for Job. His children die, his property is stolen and he suffers a terrible disease. His wife tells him to curse God and die. But Job remains faithful, even though his suffering is very great and he wishes he had never been born.

Job's friends gather round him in his trouble. From a fifteenth-century illuminated manuscript in Poitiers, France.

Friends gather round him to give him advice. They tell him that he must have done something very wrong to be punished like this. But Job knows he has done nothing to deserve such suffering, and he won't take the blame for it. Finally, Job gets very angry with God. 'Will no one listen to what I am saying? I swear that every word is true. Let Almighty God answer me… I would tell God everything I have done, and hold my head high in his presence' (Job 31:35, 37).

God replies to Job, but he doesn't really answer Job's questions. He reminds Job of the beauty and majesty of the world. He tells Job how little he knows. Job is made to feel very small. But after that, at the end of the story, Job is rewarded with a new family and new possessions, and he becomes a great man again.

The book of Job has a happy ending, but it doesn't have the answer to the question why people suffer. It presents the different characters of the story with their different points of view – Job, Job's wife, Job's friends, Satan, God – and watches them hammer out their arguments. But the argument is not won by anybody. Even the happy ending doesn't seem quite real. Job's anguished and angry cry, 'Will no one listen to what I am saying?' stays hanging in the air.

Job and Jesus

Christians do not know for sure why innocent people like Job suffer. But Christians believe one thing about God that the writer of the book of Job couldn't know about. For Christians, the story of Jesus is the story of how God lived a human life and experienced it 'from the inside'. It is the story of God understanding for himself what it means to suffer as a human being, and even to die. Jesus' cry to his Father, 'Why did you abandon me?' goes even further than Job's cry of anger. Yet even in the face of suffering and death, Jesus continues to show forgiveness and love. This idea was expressed by another 'wisdom' writer: 'Love is as powerful as death… Water cannot put it out; no flood can drown it' (Song of Songs 8:6–7).

'The ostrich leaves her eggs on the ground for the heat in the soil to warm them' (Job 39:14). God told Job to consider the wonders of the natural world.

21 A Divided Kingdom: Israel and Judah

Look it Up

The division of the kingdom:
I Kings 12

The invasion of Sennacherib:
2 Kings 18–20

Isaiah:
Chapter 24

King Solomon died in 922 BCE and was succeeded by his son Rehoboam, a young man as foolish as his father was wise. Rehoboam refused to listen to his father's advisers. He surrounded himself with his own friends who told him to treat the people harshly. As a result, the northern tribes of Israel rebelled against Rehoboam and chose their own king, Jeroboam. Only the tribes of Judah and Benjamin remained part of Rehoboam's kingdom. The northern kingdom, ruled by Jeroboam and his successors, was called Israel, and Samaria was its capital. The southern kingdom, now called Judah, was ruled by Rehoboam and his descendants in the line of King David, and its capital was Jerusalem.

Sennacherib's capture of the Judean city of Lachish. A relief from Sennacherib's palace at Nineveh.

The northern kingdom of Israel lasted just 200 years until it was conquered by the Assyrians in 722 BCE. The kings of Judah continued to reign, but often under Assyrian control, until the Babylonian conquest in 586 BCE.

The books of 1 and 2 Kings tell the story of the two kingdoms. One king, whose reign we know much about, was Hezekiah, who ruled Judah from 727 to 698 BCE. In his time, the Assyrians conquered the northern kingdom of Israel and they practically controlled the southern kingdom of Judah as well. But in 705, Hezekiah, supported by the Egyptians, rebelled against the king of Assyria, Sennacherib. Hezekiah strengthened the walls of Jerusalem, and dug a tunnel to bring water into the city in case it was attacked.

Sennacherib's account of the siege of Jerusalem

The records of the kingdom of Assyria, written on clay tablets and discovered in the Assyrian capital, Nineveh, gives Sennacherib's own account of his invasion: 'As for Hezekiah the Jew, who did not bow in submission to me… I shut up like a caged bird within Jerusalem, his royal city. The awful splendour of my lordship overwhelmed him… he sent a personal messenger to deliver the tribute and bow down like a slave.'

In 1880, two boys exploring Hezekiah's tunnel discovered this inscription from Hezekiah's time, describing how workers dug from each direction and met in the middle.

Sennacherib's army captured all the towns of Judah before arriving at Jerusalem in 701 BCE. What happened then is not very clear. Hezekiah paid the Assyrians a large amount of money and treasure. The prophet Isaiah urged Hezekiah not to surrender. The Assyrians did not capture the city and eventually went away. There was a report that thousands of Assyrian soldiers had died in their camp. The people of Judah celebrated it as a victory, but Judah was not free from the great empires that surrounded them. Before long, it was to be the turn of the Babylonians to bring Judah under their rule.

The kingdoms of Israel and Judah and their powerful neighbours – Egypt, Syria (Aram), Assyria, Babylonia.

- Assyrian control, c. 850 BCE
- Assyrian control, 710 BCE
- Assyrian gains by 650 BCE

What happened to Sennacherib's army?

The writer of 2 Kings says that the angel of God struck down the army of Sennacherib in the night. The Greek historian Herodotus, writing more than 200 years later, says that the Assyrians went on to fight the Egyptians, but that a plague of mice nibbled through all the Assyrian bowstrings and sandal straps, leaving them unable to fight. The Egyptians killed thousands of Assyrian soldiers. Herodotus says that in Egypt there was still a statue of the pharaoh, holding a mouse, and saying, 'Look on me and learn to respect the gods.'

Dates of the divided kingdom

In 2 Kings, when a king starts to reign in either Israel or Judah, the year is given of the reign of the king in the other kingdom; for example: 'In the seventh year of the reign of King Jehu of Israel, Joash became king of Judah, and he ruled in Jerusalem for 40 years' (2 Kings 12:1). This complicated way of dating the years is sometimes hard to match up with the dates of events that we know about from other sources – for instance, some of the great battles of the time. The result is some uncertainty in the dates of the period of the divided kingdom. The dates given in this book are those used by many scholars; but a different scheme of dates will be found in some other books.

'Hezekiah… built a reservoir and dug a tunnel to bring water into the city' (2 Kings 20:20). Hezekiah's tunnel in Jerusalem and the 'pool of Siloam' mentioned in John's Gospel.

22 The Early Prophets: Elijah and Elisha

Mount Carmel today, overlooking the harbor at Haifa, with a Bahá'í temple in the centre. Carmel is a holy place for Jews, Christians, Muslims and Bahá'ís.

Latin names for the prophets

The Latin for Elijah is **Elias,** and the Latin for Elisha is **Eliseus**; sometimes you will find these names used in the Bible. In the same way, Isaiah sometimes appears as **Esaias,** and Jeremiah as **Jeremias**.

Much of the Old Testament is taken up with the books of the **prophets**. A prophet is a person who speaks a message from God. Sometimes a prophet had a group of followers, who were called the 'sons of the prophet'. The kings of Israel and Judah had prophets attached to their court, and the prophets were then expected to give a message that would support the king. Many of the Old Testament prophets, however, bravely spoke messages from God that were unpopular and landed them in trouble.

Elijah

Elijah lived in the reign of King Ahab, of the northern kingdom of Israel, and Queen Jezebel. The stories of Elijah's life are told in the first book of Kings. Ahab and Jezebel worshipped Baal, one of the old gods of the land of Canaan. Jezebel had hunted down and killed many of the prophets of God, and put the prophets of Baal in their place. Elijah, faithful to God, called the prophets of Baal to meet him on Mount Carmel. He prepared a bull for sacrifice, and then he challenged the prophets of Baal to call down fire from heaven to burn it up. However hard they tried, they could not make their god answer. Then Elijah called to God, and the sacrifice burst into flames.

'Ahab… became king of Israel… He sinned against the Lord more than any of his predecessors' (1 Kings 16:29–30).

In another story, King Ahab wanted a vineyard that belonged to a man called Naboth. He wanted it so much that Queen Jezebel arranged for Naboth to be falsely accused and put to death, so that Ahab could take the vineyard for himself. Elijah went to meet Ahab in the vineyard. 'Have you caught up with me, my enemy?' asked Ahab. 'Yes, I have,' Elijah replied, and boldly criticized him for his wickedness.

Elijah is remembered throughout the Bible as the greatest of the Old Testament prophets. He stood up for those who were oppressed and ill-treated by the rich and powerful. In this he was followed by other prophets such as Amos. John the Baptist and Jesus did the same.

Elisha

Elijah called a young man named Elisha to be his disciple. The stories of Elisha are in the second book of Kings. The best-known story is about Naaman, the commander of the army of the king of Syria. Naaman suffered from the skin disease leprosy, and Elisha was known to heal the sick. Naaman arrived with his guards and with great ceremony outside Elisha's home. Elisha told him to wash in the River Jordan. At first Naaman felt insulted by the idea of doing something so humble, but then his servants pointed out to him that if Elisha had told him to do something really difficult, he would have done it. So why not do something really easy like washing in the Jordan? So Naaman changed his mind. He washed in the Jordan and was cured of his leprosy. This story was later told by Jesus to explain that God cares not only for his chosen people, but also for foreigners such as Naaman.

'Swing low, sweet chariot' is a well-known black spiritual, based on the story of Elijah going up into heaven in a 'chariot of fire'. An illustration from a thirteenth-century fresco in Anagni Cathedral, Italy.

Elijah who went up to heaven

In the story of Elijah's death in 2 Kings 2, he is taken up to heaven in a 'chariot of fire'. The prophet Malachi later spoke of Elijah returning before the 'day of the Lord'. In the time of Jesus, when people expected the Messiah, they also looked for Elijah to return. John the Baptist was asked whether he was Elijah (John 1:21). John said no, but in Matthew 11:14, Jesus said that his disciples could indeed think of John the Baptist as the 'Elijah, whose coming was predicted'. The disciple Peter said that some people thought Jesus was Elijah (Matthew 16:14). When Jesus was crucified and cried out to God in Aramaic ('Eloi, eloi…'), the soldiers thought he was calling for Elijah to come and save him.

The idea of Elijah travelling to heaven became fixed in people's minds. A book called The Apocalypse of Elijah was written in the early centuries after the time of Jesus. It imagines Elijah's time in heaven and the things he learned there about the end of the world.

23 Judgment and Mercy: Amos and Hosea

Look it Up

The story of Amos:
Amos 7

The story of Hosea:
Hosea 1–3

Amos speaks of God's judgment

The Lord says, 'I hate your religious festivals; I cannot stand them! When you bring me burnt offerings and grain offerings, I will not accept them; I will not accept the animals you have fattened to bring me as offerings. Stop your noisy songs; I do not want to listen to your harps. Instead, let justice flow like a stream, and righteousness like a river that never goes dry.'

Amos 5:21–24

A fragment of ivory furniture from the time of Amos. Amos poured scorn on those who 'lay on beds of ivory' – the height of luxury.

Amos is the earliest of the Old Testament prophets with a book to his name. He lived in the reigns of King Uzziah of Judah and King Jeroboam II of Israel (in the middle of the eighth century BCE).

Amos was not an official prophet; he didn't belong to the body of prophets attached to the royal court of either the northern or the southern kingdom. But he went to the temple of the king of Israel at Bethel and there he spoke words from God. The priest of Bethel, Amaziah, was angry and reported him to the king, telling Amos that if he wanted to speak as a prophet he should go back to the land of Judah where he came from. Amos replied that he was not an official prophet, but a herdsman and someone who looked after fig trees. 'But', he went on, 'the Lord took me from my work as a shepherd and ordered me to come and prophesy to his people Israel.'

Why did Amos's words make him so unpopular? He said that the people of Israel had behaved so badly, ill-treating the poor and making a mockery of their religion, that God would not save them from disaster. The people of Israel had always taken comfort from the fact that God had specially brought them from the Egypt to the Promised Land. But Amos said that God had also brought other peoples such as the Philistines from distant lands. It was not enough for the people of Israel to think of themselves as a chosen people: they must behave like one as well. It was not enough to come to God with music and sacrifice. 'Stop your noisy songs', said God. 'I do not want to listen to your harps. Instead, let justice flow like a stream, and righteousness like a river that never goes dry.'

Hosea lived in the northern kingdom of Israel a little later than Amos. Like Amos, he spoke of God's judgment on the kingdom for its wickedness.

Like Amos, Hosea calls for justice and right action, and religion without hypocrisy. Hosea has more to say about God's love and forgiveness than Amos does; but then, Hosea had a very different experience from Amos.

God told Hosea that Israel was behaving like a prostitute. A prostitute is someone who has sex in return for money, not out of love. The people of Israel were supposed to be people who loved God but instead they were faithless to him and were only out to make themselves rich.

God told Hosea to marry a prostitute and love her. Hosea did so. His wife's name was Gomer, and they had children. It helped Hosea to understand how God felt about Israel. The people of Israel had worshipped many different gods, but God still loved them just as Hosea loved Gomer. The people of Israel believed that the gods they worshipped had looked after them, but God said, 'I am the one who gave her the corn, the wine, the olive oil…' 'How can I give you up, Israel?' God says. 'How can I abandon you? … My heart will not let me do it! My love for you is too strong.' The message of Hosea is that God never gives up loving his people.

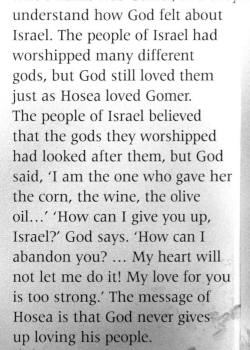

Hosea speaks of God's mercy

The Lord says, 'When Israel was a child, I loved him and called him out of Egypt as my son.

'But the more I called to him, the more he turned away from me.

'My people sacrificed to Baal; they burnt incense to idols.

'Yet I was the one who taught Israel to walk.

'I took my people up in my arms, but they did not acknowledge that I took care of them.

'I drew them to me with affection and love. I picked them up and held them to my cheek; I bent down to them and fed them.'

Hosea 11:1–4

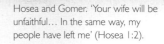

Hosea and Gomer. 'Your wife will be unfaithful… In the same way, my people have left me' (Hosea 1:2).

51

24 The Great Prophet: Isaiah

Isaiah and Jesus

The writers of the book of Isaiah had a message for their own time, but Christians have always seen it as pointing forward to Jesus as well. Passages from Isaiah are always read in churches at Christmas and on Good Friday. For Christians, it is Jesus who will be born to a young woman, and who will be called 'Immanuel' or 'God is with us' (Isaiah 7:10–14). For Christians, it is Jesus who will be 'the Prince of Peace' (Isaiah 9:1–7). It is Jesus who is the great king from the line of David (Isaiah 11:1–10). It is Jesus who is the 'Servant of the Lord' who suffered and was raised up (Isaiah 52:13 – 53:12). And it is the good news of Jesus which is the 'light' by which all people can come to know God (Isaiah 60:1–3).

The Book of Isaiah is the longest of the books of the prophets – 66 chapters altogether. Many scholars have thought that it began as two or even three books, the second and third beginning at chapter 40 and chapter 55, written by different people and later put together as one book.

The book begins: 'This book contains the messages about Judah and Jerusalem which God revealed to Isaiah son of Amoz during the time when Uzziah, Jotham, Ahaz, and Hezekiah were kings of Judah.' These four kings ruled Judah from 740 to 698 BCE. At that time, the kingdom of Judah was under threat both from the northern kingdom of Israel and from the more powerful kingdom of Aram (or Syria) still further to the north. So this part of the book of Isaiah reflects the eighth century BCE.

A famous passage in chapter 6 tells how Isaiah was in the Temple of Jerusalem and had a vision of angelic beings called the Seraphim. He heard the voice of God saying, 'Whom shall I send? Who will be our messenger?' Isaiah replied, 'I will go! Send me!' That was the start of Isaiah's work as a prophet. Isaiah himself is also mentioned in 2 Kings and 2 Chronicles.

The second half of the book is set later. Jerusalem is in ruins (52:9). The people of Israel are in exile (45:13). The enemy is Babylon (47:1). The great Persian emperor Cyrus II is spoken of as the one who will rebuild the city. Cyrus is a well-known historical figure. He conquered Babylon in 539 BCE and made it part of his empire. It was he who allowed the Jewish exiles to return from Babylon and rebuild Jerusalem. So this part of the book of Isaiah reflects the sixth century BCE, two centuries after chapters 1 to 39.

If the different parts of the book come from different writers at different times, then someone still decided to put them all together in one book. Maybe the writer of the later parts simply added them to the first part. In fact, the different parts of the book fit very well together. In this book, God warns his people to act rightly. If they rebel against him, God will not save them from the great empires that surround them. But God's mercy is even greater than his justice, the book says, and in the end he will bring his people back to their land. There will be a king from the family of David who will bring about a time of peace. There will be a 'Servant of the Lord' who will suffer greatly, but will be raised up in triumph. And the people of Israel will become a 'light' for the whole world – all the countries of the earth will come to know God through his chosen people.

The peaceful kingdom

Isaiah 11:1–9 is a vision of the beautiful kingdom that the descendant of King David will set up. 'Wolves and sheep will live together in peace,' says the prophet; 'and leopards will lie down with young goats. Calves and lion cubs will feed together, and little children will take care of them.' This is a poetic way of saying that the new king (the 'Messiah') will bring peace and reconciliation for the whole world. It is a reminder of the Garden of Eden in Genesis – the way it says God always meant the world to be.

Peace, and a little child shall lead them.
A picture of Isaiah's vision of the peaceful kingdom by William Strutt (1825–1915).

Look it Up

Jonah runs away from God:
Jonah 1

Jonah goes to Nineveh:
Jonah 3–4

What sort of story is this?

Jonah is mentioned in 2 Kings 14:25 as a historical figure, and Joppa, Tarshish and Nineveh were real places, but other things in the story are not realistic. A fish that swallows a man whole and vomits him up three days later still alive, and animals that wear sackcloth as a sign of repentance, for example – this is a story that is meant to make people laugh. Jewish people are known for their jokes and comic stories that somehow still say serious things. This Jewish writer gently pokes fun at those who want God to punish their enemies, and who never stop to think that God might want their enemies to be their friends!

Before travellers could board ship, they had to negotiate a fare with the ship's owner.

Jonah, the son of Amittai, lived in the kingdom of Israel in the reign of King Jeroboam II (786 to 746 BCE). This story, however, was probably written down much later, when the great city of Nineveh had become a distant memory.

It is the story of an unwilling prophet, a city that unexpectedly turns to God, and a God who is more merciful than angry. Although it has a serious point, the book of Jonah is full of comic detail.

God told Jonah to go to Nineveh, the capital city of the great Assyrian empire, and tell the people to turn from their wicked ways. Jonah was so alarmed by what God asked him to do that he took a ship from Joppa to the city of Tarshish – as far as possible from Nineveh in the opposite direction.

But Jonah never got to Tarshish. God sent a storm, and the ship nearly sank. The sailors, who all prayed to different gods, tried to find out which god had sent the storm. They drew lots, and the lot pointed to Jonah. Jonah knew that the storm was his fault, so he told the sailors to throw him overboard. The storm stopped, the sailors were saved – and as for Jonah, God sent a big fish to swallow him up. Three days later the fish vomited him on to dry land.

God told Jonah a second time to go and tell the people of Nineveh to repent. This time Jonah did as God said. He went to Nineveh and announced: 'In 40 days Nineveh will be destroyed!' To his great surprise, everyone took him seriously. The king ordered a fast, everyone put on sackcloth as a sign of their sorrow, and they all prayed to God. Even the animals fasted and wore sackcloth!

The sign of Jonah

The Pharisees asked Jesus for some sign to prove that he really was from God. Jesus replied that they would get no sign except 'the sign of Jonah'. Luke takes this to mean that the people of Nineveh turned to God when Jonah gave them God's message, and the people in Jesus' own day should do the same. Matthew sees another meaning in the 'sign of Jonah'. Jonah spent three days inside the fish before he came safely to land. Here is a hint of Jesus' own burial in the grave, and being brought back to life on the third day.

Matthew 12:38–42; Luke 11:29–32

So God forgave the people of Nineveh, and the city was not destroyed. Rather than being glad, Jonah actually felt that God had made a fool of him. Jonah had announced that the city would be destroyed, and it was still standing. He felt so angry and embarrassed that he wanted to die. He went out of the city and sat down to grumble at God.

But God had another lesson to teach Jonah. The sun was hot, and God made a plant grow to give him some shade. But the next day, the plant was eaten away and died. Jonah was now hot as well as cross. God pointed out to Jonah that he was getting very cross about one plant that grew up and then died. It wasn't much to be bothered about. But God was bothered about all the people of the city of Nineveh. Weren't they more important than a plant?

This story was probably written at a time when the people of Israel were in exile, or when their land was part of one of the great empires. Many scholars think it was in the fourth century BCE. The people of Israel were becoming used to mixing among people of many different races and religions – just like the sailors who all prayed to their own god. The message of the book of Jonah is that God cared for other peoples just as much as he did for Israel.

A carving of an Assyrian lion hunt in Nineveh from the reign of Ashurbanipal (669–627 BCE). The carving is now in the British Museum.

Nineveh

Nineveh became the capital of the Assyrian empire in the reign of Sennacherib (about 700 BCE) and was destroyed by the Medes and Babylonians in 612 BCE. It was founded at least 2200 BCE, on the banks of the River Tigris in what is now northern Iraq, near the modern city of Mosul. The book of Jonah says that it took three days to cross the city, though the surviving ruins are only eight miles in circumference.

Tarshish was as far west as anyone at that time could imagine it was possible to travel. Gath Hepher is mentioned in 2 Kings 14:25 as Jonah's hometown.

Look it Up

The last days of the kingdom of Judah:
2 Kings 25

Nebuchadnezzar

Nebuchadnezzar II ruled the kingdom of Babylon from 605 to 562 BCE. He was a great warrior who brought the kingdom of Babylon to its greatest period of power and prosperity. Babylon was a vast city in what is now Iraq, and has been thoroughly excavated by archaeologists. Nebuchadnezzar built three palaces that have been discovered, as well as the magnificent Ishtar Gate, which has been reconstructed in both a museum in Berlin and Babil.

The Ishtar Gate, reconstructed in Babil, modern Babylon (Iraq). The original gateway was one of the splendours of the Babylonian empire, of which Judah became a part.

Chapter 21 told how the northern kingdom of Israel was captured by the Assyrians in 722 BCE, and how Hezekiah, king of the southern kingdom of Judah, rebelled against them. At that time, people worshipped God at village shrines called 'high places'. The writers of the book of Kings praise Hezekiah for having these closed down and insisting that everyone came to Jerusalem to worship in the Temple.

Another king of Judah who changed the way people worshipped was Hezekiah's great-grandson Josiah. During his long reign from about 639 to 609 BCE, Josiah removed all traces of the worship of other gods which had gone on since the time of Solomon and before. 2 Kings 22 tells how a 'book of the Law' was discovered in the Temple. This book set out exactly how the people should worship God. The book was brought to King Josiah, who began to do what the book said.

The Christian writer Jerome in the fourth

A reconstruction of the ark of the covenant in the Temple at Jerusalem. The model is at Almog, Israel.

century CE thought it was the book of **Deuteronomy**, and most scholars have agreed with him. Deuteronomy now appears in the Old Testament as the 'fifth book of Moses'. It takes the form of a long address by Moses to the people of Israel before they entered the land of Canaan, just before Moses died. Many scholars today think that in its present form it was written in the time of Josiah or a little earlier. They see it as the work of the scribes of Jerusalem who wrote the history of the kingdom and began to collect the writings of the prophets. In fact, this was the time in which the sacred books of Israel and Judah were first collected into what eventually became the Old Testament.

The capture of Jerusalem

The kingdom of Judah had survived the attack by King Sennacherib of Assyria. Then it was the turn of the Assyrians to be defeated. The Assyrian capital Nineveh fell to the Babylonians in 612 BCE. But this was not good news for the people of Judah. An Egyptian army went to support the Assyrians, and was intercepted by the king Josiah. In 609 they met in battle at Megiddo, and Josiah was killed. His son Joahaz became king, but in his time the Egyptians conquered the land. Joahaz was taken prisoner to Egypt. The king of Egypt made Joahaz's son Jehoiakim king in Judah, but expected him to stay loyal to Egypt and pay the Egyptians a huge amount of money.

The Egyptians and the Babylonians continued to struggle for control of the region. King Nebuchadnezzar II of Babylon defeated the Egyptians at Carchemish, and Jehoiakim seized the moment to make Judah free once more. Jehoiakim died, and his son Jehoiachin succeeded him. But now Nebuchadnezzar brought his army to Jerusalem and in about 597 it was captured. Jehoiachin was taken prisoner to Babylon, along with the Jewish rulers, the educated people and the skilled workers. Among them was a priest called Ezekiel.

The Babylonians installed Jehoiachin's uncle Zedekiah as king of Judah, but he was expected to do as they told him. Zedekiah later rebelled, and the Babylonian army returned. They captured the few cities that remained in Judah and then turned their anger on Jerusalem. In about 586 the walls of the city were torn down and the Temple left in ruins. King Zedekiah was taken to Babylon. It was the end of the kingdom of Judah.

This pottery fragment found at Lachish dates from the siege itself.

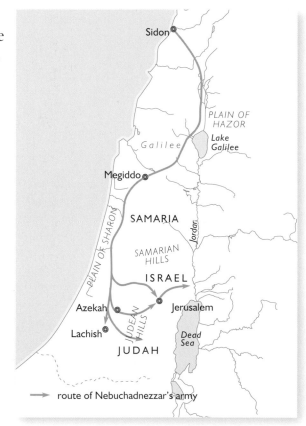

Map showing Nebuchadnezzar's invasion.

The siege of Lachish

Two of the cities captured by the Babylonian army were Lachish and Azekah (Jeremiah 34:7). Lachish was excavated in 1935 and *ostraca* from that time (pieces of clay covered in writing) were discovered. They are letters to a governor of Lachish called Hoshayahu from an officer called Yaosh who was in charge of an outpost. One speaks of a message sent by a prophet, saying, 'Take care!' Another says that they are watching for the signals from Lachish because they cannot see Azekah. They are a vivid snapshot of individuals caught up in the turmoil of a kingdom about to fall.

27 The Suffering Prophet: Jeremiah

Lamentations

The short book that follows the book of Jeremiah is called 'Lamentations' (songs of sorrow). The Lamentations are songs that mourn the ruin of the city of Jerusalem after it was captured by the Babylonians. Traditionally they are said to have been written by Jeremiah, but they are anonymous and were probably written and sung by those who remained living in Judah after many others had gone into exile.

The Lamentations begin: 'How lonely lies Jerusalem, once so full of people! … No one comes to the Temple now to worship on the holy days… The city gates stand empty… The splendour of Jerusalem is a thing of the past.'

Jeremiah lived through the dark days of the fall of Jerusalem to the Babylonians in 586 BCE. Jeremiah became a prophet as a young man in his hometown of Anathoth in the kingdom of Judah. He keenly followed international events. He knew about the defeat of the Egyptians by the Babylonians at the battle of Carchemish in 605 BCE. As a prophet, he was always trying to see what God was doing in these great events.

During the reign of the last king of Judah, Zedekiah, Jeremiah warned the king against rebelling against Babylon. The king's advisers supported the idea of a rebellion with help from the Egyptians, because they were sure that God would give them victory. King Zedekiah was torn between his advisers on the one hand and Jeremiah on the other.

The king's advisers accused Jeremiah of defecting to the Babylonians, and discouraging the soldiers of Jerusalem in their defence of the city. They had him imprisoned in a dungeon where he could have starved to death. King Zedekiah, though he didn't dare release him, moved him to a better prison.

Jeremiah's enemies were not done with him, and they insisted he must be put to death. They lowered him into a well in the palace courtyard, which was full of mud at the bottom. Once again, the king had him rescued. The king's men lifted Jeremiah out of the pit with ropes, with old rags under his armpits, and he was returned to prison. Jeremiah stayed there until Nebuchadnezzar captured Jerusalem and he was set free.

After capturing Jerusalem and taking King Zedekiah to Babylon, Nebuchadnezzar left the city in the charge of a Jewish governor, Gedaliah. But Gedaliah was assassinated by a group of Judeans who still wanted to rebel against Babylon. They escaped to Egypt, and they took Jeremiah and his secretary, a man called Baruch, with them.

Why did Jeremiah argue against a rebellion against Nebuchadnezzar? He believed that the kingdom of Judah had already rebelled against God, and so God would not save them from the Babylonians. The king of Judah lived in a fine palace, but cared little for the oppressed and poor. The official prophets who supported the king told the people that whatever the king and his nobles did, God was on their side. Jeremiah saw all this, and it made him angry. God would only be with them, said Jeremiah, if they stopped oppressing the poor, killing the innocent and worshipping false gods.

One day, Jeremiah went to a potter's house. He watched the potter at work, but the pot he was making wasn't good enough, so he began again. Jeremiah could see that God's people were like clay in God's hands. If they weren't as good as he wanted, he would have to begin again and rework them into something better. Jeremiah believed that the fall of Jerusalem was the chance for God to begin again with his people and make something better of them.

How was the book of Jeremiah written?

Jeremiah 36 tells how Baruch, Jeremiah's secretary, wrote down on scrolls all the 'oracles' (messages) that God had given him about the kingdom of Judah and the surrounding nations. Later Baruch read these out in the Temple, which got him into trouble with King Jehoiakim, who cut up the scroll with his penknife and threw it on the fire. Baruch later wrote out the words of Jeremiah on a new scroll. This chapter gives a vivid picture of how the words of the prophets were written down and collected by their followers.

The book of Jeremiah as we now have it is a patchwork of Jeremiah's oracles, much of which is written as poetry, and prose passages which tell the story of his life. It is likely that Baruch the secretary started writing these sections, though they show signs of being rewritten by others as well.

'He told me to put the rags under my arms, so that the ropes wouldn't hurt me. I did this, and they pulled me up out of the well' (Jeremiah 38:12–13).

'I went there [to the potter's house] and saw the potter working at his wheel' (Jeremiah 18:3).

28 The Visionary Prophet: Ezekiel

The book of Ezekiel and the book of Revelation

Ezekiel's vision of the river flowing out of the Temple echoes the story of the Garden of Eden in the book of Genesis. There are also echoes of it in the book of Revelation, at the end of the New Testament. But there are differences between the three pictures as well. In Genesis, a river flows out of the Garden of Eden to bring water to the whole earth. In Ezekiel's vision, instead of flowing out of the Garden of Eden, the water flows out of the Temple, because for Ezekiel it is the Temple, not the Garden of Eden, which is the place where men and women are at home with God. In the book of Revelation there is no Temple in the city, 'because its temple is the Lord God Almighty and the Lamb.' God has become fully at home with his people so that they no longer need a special place to meet him.

Ezekiel was a priest who was among those taken into exile by Nebuchadnezzar after the first Babylonian invasion of Judah in 597 BCE. He settled in a place called Tel Abib on the river Chebar, southeast of Babylon. In exile, Ezekiel began to see extraordinary visions. He then began to speak to his fellow exiles, giving them God's message from his visions. God told him that he was a 'watchman' or a 'sentinel' for his people.

In Ezekiel 1–24, the prophet speaks against the city of Jerusalem, which at that time had not finally fallen to the Babylonians. In 25–32 he speaks against the nations who had been glad to see Jerusalem captured. In 33–48 he tells how God will one day restore his people to their home.

In Ezekiel 36, God promises to gather his people from all the lands to which they had been dispersed. 'I will take you from every nation and country and bring you back to your own land,' he says. 'I will sprinkle clean water on you… I will give you a new heart and a new mind. I will take away your stubborn heart of stone and give you an obedient heart.'

One of Ezekiel's visions was of a valley full of dry bones.

The heavenly Jerusalem as described in the book of Revelation, showing the walls with precious stones, the four living creatures, and Jesus as the Lamb of God. From a twelfth-century manuscript now in the Bodleian Library in Oxford, England.

God told him to speak to the bones, and the bones began to connect again. They became covered with flesh and skin, they started to breathe, and they stood up on their feet, a great army. It was a vision of the people of Israel, destroyed by the Babylonians, becoming a nation once again.

In Ezekiel 47, he paints a magnificent picture of the Temple in Jerusalem, from which an enormous river flows, bringing fresh water to the desert, and making trees grow. The trees give food to the people, and their leaves have healing powers. It is a vision of how one day God would bring his people back to their land, and they would be bringers of peace and happiness to the whole world.

The good shepherd

In Ezekiel 34, the prophet calls the leaders of the people 'shepherds' and says that they are bad shepherds who do not care about their sheep. One day, says Ezekiel, God himself will look after his people and be their shepherd: 'I myself will look for my sheep and take care of them… I will bring them back from all the places where they were scattered on that dark, disastrous day… I will lead them back to the mountains and streams of Israel and will feed them in pleasant pastures… I myself will be the shepherd of my sheep.' In the Gospels of Matthew and Luke, Jesus echoes the vision of Ezekiel with the story of a shepherd who went in search of one lost sheep, and in the Gospel of John Jesus calls himself the 'good shepherd'.

Ezekiel in the Valley of the Dry Bones, from a painting by John Roddam Spencer Stanhope (1829–1908).

29 Exile and Return

The feast of Shelters

The feast of Shelters (in some translations 'Booths' or 'Tabernacles') is called Sukkot in Hebrew and is one of the three great annual festivals of the Old Testament. The others are the Passover (Pesach – see chapter 11) and the feast of Weeks (Shavnot). Celebrated in the early autumn, the feast of Shelters marked the end of the corn and grape harvest. The book of Leviticus (23:39–43) orders the people to gather the branches of trees and make them into shelters to live in during the week-long festival, to remind them of the time when they were travelling through the desert. The book of Nehemiah tells how the festival was revived after Jerusalem had been rebuilt (see Nehemiah 8:13–18). Jewish people still celebrate Sukkot today.

When the Babylonians invaded the kingdom of Judah and captured Jerusalem in about 597 BCE, King Jehoiachin was taken prisoner to Babylon, along with the Jewish rulers, the educated people and the skilled workers. More people were 'deported' (taken away) to Babylon about nine years later, when Jerusalem was destroyed. The time that followed is called the 'exile'. The thousands of Jewish people who had been taken to Babylon thought sadly of their homeland and longed to return.

Psalm 137 is a lament for the city which they had left behind (Jerusalem is here called Zion):

By the rivers of Babylon we sat down;
there we wept when we remembered Zion.

On the willows nearby we hung up our harps.

Those who captured us told us to sing; they told us to entertain them: 'Sing us a song about Zion.'

How can we sing a song to the Lord in a foreign land?

May I never be able to play the harp again if I forget you, Jerusalem!

May I never be able to sing again if I do not remember you, if I do not think of you as my greatest joy!

Jeremiah wrote a letter to the Jewish people in Babylon. He urged them to settle down there and not to think of being able to return at once. He told them that God was saying to them, 'Work for the good of the cities where I have made you go as prisoners… because if they are prosperous, you will be prosperous too.' Jeremiah said that after 70 years, God would allow his people to return to Jerusalem.

In fact, it came earlier than that. Less than 50 years after the fall of Jerusalem, it was Babylon's turn to fall. Cyrus, king of Persia, captured it in 539 BCE, and all the countries which Nebuchadnezzar had conquered now became part of the Persian empire. Cyrus was a wise and tolerant ruler who cared for all the peoples under his rule. In 538, he allowed Jewish people in Babylon to begin to return to Jerusalem and even to rebuild the Temple. When the new Temple was dedicated, some of the people shouted for joy, while others who remembered the old Temple wept.

After their exile and return, much had to be done to reorganize the religion of the Jews. Not only was the 'Second' Temple built and dedicated, but the holy books were collected and some were rewritten. The two books of Chronicles retell much of the books of Samuel and Kings, with the Temple given a particular importance. Much of the book of Leviticus reflects this period as well, though some of the book goes back to much earlier times. The period of the Second Temple was a time when God's chosen people, returned at last to their Promised Land, were once again confident that God cared for them and were anxious to offer him the best worship that they could.

The Cyrus Cylinder, discovered in 1879 in the ruins of the temple of the god Marduk in Babylon. It announces the fact that the exiled people, including the Jews, could return to their own country.

Nehemiah and Ezra

There are two books that tell of the return from the exile. One describes the rebuilding of the Temple by a priest called Ezra. The other describes the rebuilding of the walls of Jerusalem by Nehemiah, a Jewish man who had been cup-bearer to King Artaxerxes, a successor to Cyrus, in Babylon. It is difficult to fit the books of Ezra and Nehemiah together and to work out whether the building of the walls or the building of the Temple came first.

Cyrus the great king

An inscription from Babylon describes how Cyrus settled exiled peoples back in their homelands and gave them the temples of their gods again: 'I am Cyrus, king of the world, great king, mighty king, king of Babylon, king of the four quarters… The holy cities beyond the Tigris whose sanctuaries had been in ruins over a long period, and the gods whose abode is in the midst of them, I returned to their places and housed them in lasting abodes. I gathered together all their inhabitants and restored to them their dwellings.'

30 Tales from Captivity: Esther and Daniel

The festival of Purim

The festival of Purim is one of the festivals of the Jewish religion today. It celebrates the story of Esther. The word *purim* means a lottery, and it recalls the story that the day on which all the Jews were to be killed was to be decided by drawing lots. The story of Esther is retold at this festival, and when Haman's name is mentioned it is drowned out with special noise-makers. The festival occurs in March or April.

The festival of Purim celebrated in Israel today.

There is a wealth of stories about Jewish heroes – both men and women – during the time of Jewish exile in foreign lands. They tell of the wisdom and courage of the Jews, and how they often got the better of their foreign rulers.

The book of Esther

This book, perhaps from the fourth century BCE, tells how King Ahasuerus of Persia (usually thought to be Xerxes I) took the beautiful young woman Esther to be his queen, without realizing that she was Jewish. A man called Haman made a plot to kill all the Jews in the kingdom. Esther was desperate to save them all, but even the queen was not allowed to approach the king unless he had invited her. Greatly daring, she went to the king, and he received her kindly. She was able to turn the tables on Haman, and have him put to death instead. The story of Esther is one of several about strong and courageous Jewish women. Others told about Deborah, whose story is told in the book of Judges, and Judith, whose story is in the Apocrypha.

Archers in the palace of Darius the Great (548–486 BCE) at Susa, in what is now Iran. Susa is the setting of the story of Esther.

The book of Daniel

Daniel in the lions' den is one of the best-known stories in the Bible. But who was Daniel, and what was he doing there?

The book of Daniel is set in the time of the exile to Babylon but it is hard to match up much of the story with what is known of the history of that time. Many scholars take the view that in its present form the book comes from the time of the Maccabaean Revolt and that the king in Daniel 11 is a coded reference to Antiochus IV Epiphanes.

The book tells of Daniel and his friends at the court of Nebuchadnezzar. Like in the story of Joseph, he is a brave young Jewish man, trusting the God of his own people, outwitting the king's officials, and telling the king the meaning of his dreams. Daniel's friends, Shadrach, Meshach and Abednego, refuse to worship the king, and they are thrown into a burning, fiery furnace from which, however, they emerge uninjured.

A later king, Belshazzar, has his defeat and the destruction of the kingdom foretold by Daniel, who reads strange words written on a wall of the king's palace. This gives us the phrase 'the writing on the wall', meaning that the end is near.

Then King Darius of Media conquers Babylon. He honours Daniel with a position of great authority (again, like Joseph) but Daniel's enemies invent a law to make everyone worship the king for one month. Daniel refuses. He is thrown into the lions' den, from which he comes out alive.

The later chapters of the book of Daniel are made up of some strange visions that resemble the book of Ezekiel. This kind of writing is called 'apocalyptic' (from the Greek word for 'revelation'). Much of it is hard to make sense of, but certain things are clear. The message of the book is a promise that however hard things become for God's people, God will indeed see them through. There will be 'a time of troubles, the worst since nations first came into existence.' Daniel 12 describes how 'many of those who have already died will live again: some will enjoy eternal life, and some will suffer eternal disgrace. The wise leaders will shine with all the brightness of the sky. And those who have taught many people to do what is right will shine like the stars for ever.'

Although the book of Daniel is placed in the middle of the Old Testament, these are among the last words of the Old Testament to have been written. They are full of hope that God will give his people peace at last, and that even the dead will be raised to share in God's new kingdom.

Mene, mene, tekel, parsin ('number, number, weight, divisions')... the Hebrew words that appeared on the wall, announcing the destruction of Belshazzar's empire.

31 Warnings and Promises: More Prophets

There are nine prophets with books named after them which so far have not been mentioned. This chapter makes a brief survey of them all. They lived at different times before and after the exile.

Joel

The book of Joel tells of a plague of locusts which the prophet took to be God's punishment. Joel makes a stirring call for people to turn back to God, which Christians have often read on Ash Wednesday. He also paints a picture of the day when God would pour out his Spirit on his people. This passage (2:28–32) was used by Peter on the day of Pentecost to explain what God was doing at that moment.

Obadiah

The shortest book in the Old Testament is an oracle (or message from God) directed against the neighbouring land of Edom. The Edomites were said to have helped the Babylonians in the capture of Jerusalem.

Nahum

The prophet Nahum was writing before the fall of Nineveh in 612 BCE, and speaks against the Assyrian kingdom.

Micah

The prophet Micah lived in the reign of King Hezekiah, and he is mentioned in the book of Jeremiah as having come to Jerusalem then. The most famous passage in the book is Micah 4, which paints a picture of a people at peace, with swords and spears beaten into farming tools, when no one shall learn how to wage war, and everyone will live in peace 'among his own vineyards and fig trees, and no one will make him afraid.'

Habakkuk

This short book emphasizes the importance of trusting God, even when things go wrong: 'Even though the fig-trees have no fruit and no grapes grow on the vines, even though the olive crop fails and the fields produce no corn, even though the sheep all die and the cattle stalls are empty, I will still be joyful and glad, because the Lord God is my saviour.'

'Let us beat our swords into ploughshares.' This statue depicting the verse from Micah was made by the Russian sculptor Evgeny Vuchetich in 1959. It is at the headquarters of the United Nations in New York.

'There is no rain and nothing can grow' (Haggai 1:10). In the background stands the unfinished Temple.

Zephaniah

Zephaniah lived in the reign of Josiah. The prophet speaks out against Judah and Jerusalem in the hope that they will turn back to God. He warns them that God will bring a terrible 'day' of judgment and anger on his people. The Latin words of Zephaniah 1:15 ('it will be a day of fury') are *dies irae, dies illa*. They are used in a medieval Christian hymn called the *Dies Irae* that describes the day of judgment at the end of the world.

Haggai

The prophet Haggai lived at a time when people had begun to return from exile, but before the Temple had been rebuilt. He attacks those who have built fine homes for themselves in Jerusalem without a care for the house of God. 'You have sown much corn, but have harvested very little,' he says to them. 'You have food to eat, but not enough to make you full… Can't you see why this has happened? Now go up into the hills, get timber, and rebuild the Temple; then I will be pleased and will be worshipped as I should be.'

Malachi

Malachi is not the name of the prophet but the Hebrew word for 'messenger'. God says that he will send his 'messenger' to prepare the way for God himself to come to his people. On that day, God will punish those who deserve it, but 'for you who obey me, my saving power will rise on you like the sun and bring healing like the sun's rays.' Christians see in these words a hint of the resurrection of Jesus. 'Malachi' also says that God will send Elijah to prepare his people for his coming.

Zechariah

Like Haggai, Zechariah lived after the return from exile. His prophecies, like those of Ezekiel, take the form of strange visions; like Ezekiel, too, much of what he writes is reworked in the book of Revelation in the New Testament. His most famous oracle (or message) concerns the king who will come to Jerusalem one day, 'triumphant and victorious, but humble and riding on a donkey.' This is the picture which Jesus deliberately acted out when he rode into Jerusalem (see chapter 55).

32 Collecting the Books of the Old Testament

Look it Up

The books included in the list of Apocrypha or 'deuterocanonical' books differ between Bibles.

The pseudepigrapha

As well as the 'apocryphal' or 'deuterocanonical' books, other Jewish writings have survived from the last two centuries BCE and the first three centuries CE. These books are sometimes called the 'pseudepigrapha' ('books with a false title') because many of them were written in the name of some Old Testament figure. For instance, a book called 'The Testaments of the Twelve Patriarchs' (about 150 BCE, perhaps at the same time as the books of Daniel) claims to be the last utterances of the twelve sons of Jacob.

Not included in the Bible, these books give a lively glimpse of the religious imagination of the Jewish people in this period.

By the third century BCE, there were Jewish people living in many lands as well as the land of Israel or Judah, and Greek had become a language that many different peoples used to communicate with each other. At that time, Jewish scholars in Alexandria in Egypt translated the Hebrew Bible into Greek. There is a legend that this was at the command of the king of Egypt, who wanted to have the books of Moses in his library. The same legend says that there were 70 (or 72) scholars engaged in the translation, which is sometimes called the 'Septuagint' (from the Greek word for '70'). More often it is simply called 'the Greek Bible'.

Many copies of the Old Testament are printed with 39 books; but there are more books than that in the Septuagint or Greek version. For the Jews of Alexandria, the holiest part of the collection was the five 'books of Moses', then the 'prophets' and after that the 'writings'. But it wasn't clear which books belonged to the 'writings' and which didn't.

After the fall of Jerusalem and the destruction of the Temple in 70 CE, the Jews of Palestine (Palestine was the name given by the Greeks to the land of Israel or Judah) reorganized their religion around their local places of worship (called synagogues). As the sacrifices were no longer offered in the Temple, the reading of scripture became an even more important part of their religion, and they needed to know exactly which were their holy books. They eventually settled on the 39 books that are the ones found in most copies of the Old Testament (though they counted some together and made it 24). The list of books that make up the Old Testament is called the 'Canon' (the Greek word for 'rule').

Long before 70 CE, the other books that are in the Septuagint were well known to Christians, especially to those like Paul who could read Greek. None of these books is directly quoted in the New Testament, though passages in the book of the 'Wisdom of Solomon' are very close to parts of Paul's letters. In the second, third and fourth centuries CE, these books were read and quoted by Christians in the same way as they read and quoted the books of the Old Testament.

Jerome's translation

Jerome was a Bible scholar who lived in the fourth century CE. He made a new translation of the Bible into Latin (traditionally called the 'Vulgate'). He thought that Christians should only include in the Old Testament the books which the Jews of Palestine settled on after 70 CE.

He called the other books the 'Apocrypha' (the Greek word for 'hidden'). Augustine, another important Bible scholar who lived at the same time as Jerome, took the opposite view and included all those books in the Bible. In practice, Christians followed Augustine and took little notice of Jerome's distinction until the time of the Reformation in the sixteenth century.

After the Reformation, the different churches took different views. Some editions of the Bible today print just the 39 books of the Old Testament and the 27 books of the New Testament. Others add some of the 'apocryphal' books (sometimes also called the 'deuterocanonical' books) and these may be placed among the books of the Old Testament, or placed in a section of their own between the Old and New Testaments.

There has never been complete agreement among all Christian churches about this. There is agreement about the main books, but there are differences about where to draw a line around them.

Ulrich Zwingli (1484–1531) was one of the leaders of the sixteenth-century Reformation.

The logo of the World Council of Churches.

Different churches

Since the time of Jesus, different churches (groups of Christians) have grown up. Sometimes Christians became divided because they lived in different countries, spoke different languages, had different customs and found it hard to understand each other. Sometimes there have been bitter disagreements about Christian beliefs. Between 500 and 1000 CE, the Greek-speaking Eastern Church and the Latin-speaking Western Church gradually grew apart from each other. In the sixteenth century, the Reformation divided the church in western Europe – divisions which were later reflected in other parts of the world. There is however a big movement today towards reconciling and reuniting the Christian churches (called the 'ecumenical' movement). Much of this is done by the World Council of Churches. The WCC fosters dialogue between churches, and helps them to do joint practical work, tackling hunger, poverty and racism. Many Christians believe that what Christians have in common is more important than what divides them.

33 Discovering the 'Hidden' Books

Look it Up

The praise of godly people:
Ecclesiasticus (Sirach) 44:1–7

The souls of the righteous:
Wisdom of Solomon 3:1–3

The praise of godly people

So let us now give praise to godly men, our ancestors of generations past, men whom the Lord honoured with great glory, in whom his greatness has been seen from the beginning of time. There were some who ruled kingdoms, and some who were known for their strength. Some were wise advisers, and some spoke prophecies. There were statesmen whose policies governed the people, rulers who issued decrees, scholars who spoke wise words, and those who used pointed proverbs, poets, and composers of music, rich and powerful men living peacefully at home. All these were famous in their own times, honoured by the people of their day.

Ecclesiasticus (Sirach) 44:1–7

Tobias and the angel: a picture by Andrea del Verocchio (1435–1486), now in the National Gallery, London. Tobias is shown wearing the clothes of the artist's own time.

Even if there is no complete agreement among all Christian churches about which books are 'canonical' or 'apocryphal' or 'deuterocanonical', all these books are part of the Christian heritage.

The book of Tobit

This tale was probably first written in Aramaic in the second century BCE. It tells how a man called Tobit was taken into exile in Nineveh after the Assyrians had conquered the kingdom of Israel, where he went blind. He remembered he had once hidden a fortune in the neighbouring land of Media, and sent his son Tobias to find it. Tobias is accompanied by his dog and the angel Raphael. Tobias marries a girl called Sarah (who is bothered by a demon). He deals with the demon, finds the money, and returns to Tobit, who is healed by Raphael. Medieval and Renaissance artists loved this story.

The book of Judith

Judith is a courageous Jewish heroine in the style of Deborah and Jael. The story is inaccurate in its history and was most likely meant to be read simply as an exciting tale. It was probably written in the first century BCE, and it tells how Judith trapped and beheaded an Assyrian general called Holofernes, who had not only invaded the land, but tried to seduce her. It is another story the artists loved.

The rest of the book of Esther

These are chapters of Esther found in the Greek or Septuagint version but not in the original Hebrew. It adds to the religious character of the book, as the main part of the book of Esther never mentions God!

The Wisdom of Solomon

This big book was by a Jewish writer who knew about Greek philosophy, and who could write about his faith in a way that would make sense to other people familiar with Greek thought. Some of its ideas are close to John's Gospel, Paul's letters and the letter to the Hebrews. Paul may well have known it, and some early Christians regarded it as part of the New Testament rather than the Old. It was probably written early in the first century CE, and is certainly not by Solomon.

Ecclesiasticus, or the Wisdom of Jesus, Son of Sirach

This is another long book, called either 'Ecclesiasticus' or 'Sirach' for short. It is important not to confuse it with Ecclesiastes, a book in the Old Testament. 'Jesus, son of Sirach' is the name of the author, though his name is often used in its Hebrew form, Ben Sira. Ben Sira wrote the book in Hebrew in the second century BCE, and his grandson translated it into Greek, as he says at the beginning. The book is in the tradition of Jewish 'wisdom', with many proverbs. Chapter 44, beginning 'So let us now give praise to godly men…', is often read in churches.

The story of Judith beheading Holofernes (Judith 13) is one of the stories from the so-called 'hidden' books of the Bible.

Baruch, and the letter of Jeremiah

The book of Baruch claims to be by Jeremiah's secretary but was probably written in the second century BCE. The letter of Jeremiah, like Baruch, is an addition to the story of Jeremiah, and is sometimes counted as chapter 6 of Baruch.

The rest of the book of Daniel

The Prayer of Azariah, the Song of the Three Young Men, the story of Susanna, and the story Bel and the Dragon are all additions to the Greek version of the book of Daniel.

The first and second books of the Maccabees

These important books are looked at in chapter 34.

The first book of Esdras

Esdras is Greek for the name Ezra, and this book is a retelling of the books of Ezra and Nehemiah from the second century BCE. Other 'apocryphal' books are the **Prayer of Manasseh**, **Psalm 151**, **3 Maccabees** and **4 Maccabees**, and **2 Esdras**, which are accepted by some churches but which are largely unknown and seldom read.

34 The Maccabean Revolt

One of the most powerful rulers of the ancient world was Alexander the Great. He was the king of Macedon in Greece, and in 334 BCE he set out to conquer the great Persian empire, which by that time ruled all the lands of the Bible. Alexander took Egypt from the Persians, and founded there the city of Alexandria. His army marched as far as India. Although this vast area did not outlast the death of Alexander as one empire, Greek language and culture became widespread. Educated people were attracted to Greek customs and ideas.

The region of Syria and Palestine was ruled by a family called the Seleucids, descended from one of Alexander's generals. One of them, King Antiochus IV Epiphanes, began a campaign to make the Jews give up their religion in favour of the Greek gods. He ordered sacrifices to be offered to the gods in every Jewish town, and built an altar to Zeus in the Temple at Jerusalem.

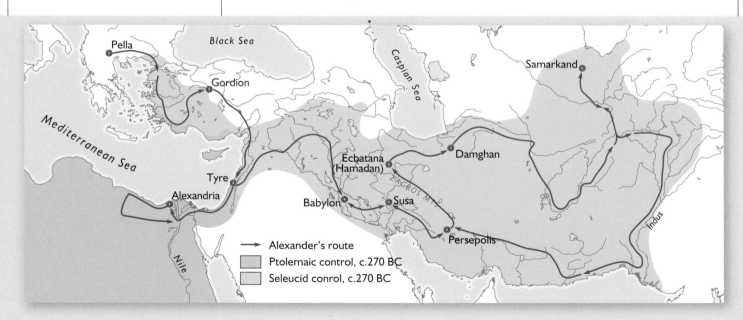

Alexander's route

Ptolemaic control, c.270 BC

Seleucid conrol, c.270 BC

Alexander the Great and his successors

If scholars are right that Daniel 11 is a coded picture of the break-up of the empire of Alexander the Great (see chapter 30), then the fourth king, 'richer than all the others' is Xerxes I who ruled 486–465 BCE who tried to conquer Greece ('he will challenge the kingdom of Greece') and defeated the Spartans at the battle of Thermopylae in 480 BCE. A warrior king (Alexander) then 'will rule over a huge empire and do whatever he wants' (he took his armies as far as India). But his kingdom is broken and divided, though not among his descendants (Alexander died at the age of 33, and his conquests were shared out among his generals). What Daniel 11 calls 'the king of Egypt' was Ptolemy, who founded the dynasty who ruled Egypt until the Romans conquered. The 'king of Syria' refers to the Seleucid family who ruled Persia, Syria and Palestine. And finally there is a king who is 'an evil man who has no right to be king… He will boast that he is greater than any god… But he will die, with no one there to help him' – a coded picture of King Antiochus IV Epiphanes.

Judas Maccabaeus recaptures the Temple in Jerusalem.

The first book of Maccabees tells the story of the revolt of faithful Jews against Antiochus in 167 BCE. They were led by an old priest called Mattathias and his sons. After Mattathias died, his son Judas 'Maccabaeus' (the name means 'the hammer') led the revolt. Judas was a brilliant general, and under his command a Jewish army defeated the forces of Antiochus and captured Jerusalem. The altar of Zeus was destroyed and the Temple rededicated.

In 161 Judas was killed in battle, but his brothers continued the war. The last brother, Simon, became high priest and ruler of the Jews. The family of Mattathias is known both as the 'Maccabees' and the 'Hasmonaeans'. The line of rulers begun by Simon is called the Hasmonaean dynasty.

The writer of 1 Maccabees is concerned to show that the heroes of the Maccabean Revolt stand in the tradition of Old Testament faithful warriors like Joshua, Gideon and David. Like the Maccabees themselves, the writer believes passionately in Jewish faith, law and custom. Other writings such as the Wisdom of Solomon or Ecclesiasticus emphasize the similarity of Greek and Jewish thinking. 1 Maccabees emphasizes the difference, and it had an important influence on the mood of the Jewish people at the time Jesus was born and brought up.

The second book of Maccabees is not the sequel to the first, but a collection of other writings about the Maccabean Revolt. They include stories of Jews willing to be tortured and killed rather than give up their faith.

The feast of Hanukkah

The rededication of the Temple of Jerusalem in 164 BCE is celebrated by an annual festival called Hanukkah. It is also called the 'festival of lights', because candles are lit to remember the relighting of the lamps in the Temple. In John 10, Jesus visits the Temple at Hanukkah (called in John's Gospel the 'festival of dedication').

The festival of Hanukkah, celebrated by a Jewish family today.

35 What is the New Testament?

What is a testament?

The word 'testament', often used in older English translations of the Bible, is usually translated as 'covenant' in the more modern versions. A testament or covenant is a bond or binding agreement. People can make covenants with each other, like the bond of friendship that David made with Jonathan (1 Samuel 18). But more importantly, the bond between the people of Israel and their God is called the 'covenant'. God promised to guard and protect his people, and the people promised to keep his Law.

The prophet Jeremiah spoke of a 'new covenant' that God would make one day with his people. When Jesus ate the Last Supper with his disciples and gave them bread and wine to be his body and blood, he spoke of the 'new covenant'. So Christians speak of the time up to Jesus as the time of the 'old covenant' or 'Old Testament', and the time from Jesus onwards as the time of the 'new covenant' or 'New Testament'.

The New Testament is much shorter than the Old. Rather than telling the story of the people of Israel over hundreds of years, the New Testament tells the story of one man and a few of his first followers. For Christians this is the most important story in the Bible, but it cannot be understood without knowing much of the Old Testament first.

These are the books of the New Testament:

The Gospels and the Acts of the Apostles
The Gospel according to Matthew
The Gospel according to Mark
The Gospel according to Luke
The Gospel according to John
The Acts of the Apostles

Matthew, Mark, Luke and John are the four people traditionally thought to have written the four Gospels. The reasons for this will be discussed in chapters 45–47 and 49. The names of the Gospels are often shortened, e.g. 'the Gospel of Matthew', or 'Matthew's Gospel' or just 'Matthew'.

The four Gospels tell the story of the life, death and resurrection of Jesus Christ. There is overlap between them, but each writer tells the story in their own way. The Acts of the Apostles (a sequel to the Gospel of Luke) tells how the first followers of Jesus, especially Peter and Paul, took the message of Jesus out into the Roman world.

The Letters:
Paul's Letters
Letter to the Romans
First Letter to the Corinthians
Second Letter to the Corinthians
Letter to the Galatians
Letter to the Ephesians
Letter to the Philippians
Letter to the Colossians
First Letter to the Thessalonians
Second Letter to the Thessalonians
First Letter to Timothy
Second Letter to Timothy
Letter to Titus
Letter to Philemon

Other Letters

Letter to the Hebrews
Letter of James
First Letter of Peter
Second Letter of Peter
First Letter of John
Second Letter of John
Third Letter of John
Letter of Jude

The Letters were written to teach and encourage groups of Christians in living the Christian life. Most of them are by Paul to the Christian communities (or 'churches') which he had founded or visited.

The Revelation to John

The Revelation (or 'Apocalypse') was written to encourage Christians especially during times of persecution.

This is the order in which the books are printed in the Bible. It means that Jesus is read about first, followed by books that describe the life of the earliest Christians and their communities. This order is a logical one, but it is not the only way to read the New Testament. Like the Old Testament, the books that come first in this order were not the first to be written. Paul's letters had probably all been finished before the Gospels were started.

   The following chapters will look at the story of Jesus first and the times he lived in. The chapters after that will look at the first followers of Jesus, especially Paul, the first Christian to leave any writings behind him. Then all the books of the New Testament will be looked at in turn, as well as some other early Christian writings that aren't in the New Testament. The last chapters will piece together what the New Testament says about Jesus – his birth, his teaching, his crucifixion and his resurrection from the dead.

Greek, the language of the New Testament

After the conquests of Alexander the Great, Greek language and culture spread right across the lands of the Bible. Some of the books of the Apocrypha and all the books of the New Testament were written in this version of Greek. It is a simple version of the language, called *koiné* (common) Greek, used by peoples across the eastern Mediterranean by peoples who still had their own languages. Jesus would have heard at least four languages as he grew up: Hebrew, the language of the Bible; Aramaic, the language he probably spoke at home; Latin, the language of the Roman government and army and their officials; and Greek, the language of learning and ideas, as well as the most convenient one for business and commerce between one country and another. In some versions of Luke's Gospel, it is said that the accusation against Jesus (that he claimed to be the king of the Jews), which was pinned to his cross, was written in Latin, Greek and Hebrew (or Aramaic).

Writing materials in New Testament times.

36 The Roman World

Look it Up

The story of the centurion at Capernaum:
Luke 7:1–10

Jesus on trial before Pontius Pilate:
Mark 15:1–20

Paul is taken as prisoner to Rome:
Acts 27–28

Paul writes from a prison cell:
Philippians 1:3–14

The books of the Old Testament were written at different times and different places. But the books of the New Testament were all written within a few decades of each other. With the possible exception of the author of Luke and Acts, who may have been a Gentile Christian, the New Testament writers were all Jewish Christians, living in the Roman empire.

Roman power had steadily grown in the five centuries before Jesus. By the time of Jesus, the Romans ruled all the lands around the Mediterranean, from France and Spain in the west to Egypt and Syria in the east. The Romans invaded Britain in 43 CE and made it a province, and in the second century CE expanded further into eastern Europe as well as Armenia and Mesopotamia.

The Roman empire in the first century CE.

The Romans are never far away in the stories told about Jesus. For example, Luke's Gospel tells the story of the journey of Joseph and Mary to Bethlehem, where Jesus was born. Luke says that the journey had to be made because the emperor Augustus had ordered a census (a count) of all the people in the empire. (Such censuses were ordered by the emperors.) Later on, those who opposed Jesus' teaching tried to trap him into saying whether taxes should be paid to the emperor or not. Later still, when Jesus was found guilty before a Jewish court in

Jerusalem, he then had to be sent to the Roman governor, Pontius Pilate, because only the Romans could pass the death sentence. Jesus was crucified by Roman soldiers.

The Romans are not always shown as the enemies of Jesus. Luke's Gospel tells of a kind and generous centurion who had built a synagogue (a Jewish place of worship) in the town of Capernaum. When his favourite servant fell ill, it was the Jewish elders of the town who begged Jesus to help the centurion. This shows that even though the Romans were the occupying forces of Palestine, it was possible for individual Romans to be on good terms with the local Jewish population.

The Letters and the Acts of the Apostles show how the followers of Jesus, after his lifetime, travelled around the Roman empire, spreading the message of Jesus. Paul was arrested by Roman soldiers and sent under armed guard to Rome to be tried before the emperor himself. (That was Paul's privilege because he had been born a Roman citizen.) Two Roman governors, Felix and Festus, mentioned in the Acts of the Apostles, are also mentioned by the Jewish historian Josephus.

The Revelation of John was written to encourage communities of Christians at a time when they were facing persecution from the Roman government. There were such periods of persecution during the reigns of Nero (54–68 CE) and Domitian (81–96 CE). The Roman writer Pliny the Younger (61–112 CE), who was the governor of Bythinia, wrote letters to his friend Emperor Trajan about the difficulties he was having with Christians who refused to give up their faith.

Emperor Augustus

The Romans come to Palestine

The Romans are first mentioned in the Bible in 1 Maccabees 8, where Judas Maccabaeus is told 'about the wars the Romans had fought and their heroic acts among the Gauls.' Judas decided that the Romans would be their best ally against Antiochus IV Epiphanes and sent ambassadors to Rome to make a treaty. At that time, the Romans were expanding their empire into the eastern Mediterranean. The Roman general Pompey conquered Syria and in 63 BCE he made Palestine part of that province. Herod was made governor of Galilee in 37 BCE, and then, in 40 BCE, 'King of the Jews'.

Roman soldiers overlooking the Temple in Jerusalem from their garrison, the Antonia Fortress.

37 Palestine in the Time of Jesus

Look it Up

A story about a Samaritan:
Luke 10:25–37

A story about a Pharisee and a tax collector:
Luke 18:9–14

The Dead Sea Scrolls

Between 1947 and 1960, hundreds of scrolls were discovered in caves at Qumran near the Dead Sea. The scrolls include books of the Old Testament and others not known about before. The earliest date from 200 BCE and the latest from 70 CE. The scrolls belonged to a Jewish community living at Qumran, and they say much about this community. They hoped for the coming of *two* Messiahs. They used many of the same phrases that are found in the Gospels. They called themselves the 'people of light', a phrase Jesus also used in his parables. This does not mean that Jesus belonged to the Qumran community, or that the Qumran community followed Jesus. It does help to show how the Gospels belong to their time. The Qumran scrolls show how some Jews thought and spoke and acted in Palestine in the first century CE.

Caves at Qumran. It was in these caves that the 'Dead Sea Scrolls' were discovered.

The Romans who occupied the land of the Jewish people called it *Palestina* or Palestine, after the Philistines who had lived there in Old Testament times. The Jewish people themselves called the southern area of the land, surrounding Jerusalem, Judah, or, in Latin, *Judaea*. This was a smaller area than the old southern kingdom of Judah. The northern area where Jesus grew up was called Galilee. Galilee is green and fertile, and it borders on the Sea of or Lake Galilee (also called the Sea of Tiberias, or Gennesaret). Judaea, which reaches down to the Dead Sea, is dry and barren. The Judaean wilderness, between Jerusalem and Jericho, where Jesus set his story of the Good Samaritan, is very desolate.

There were many religious groups among the Jews at the time of Jesus. They could be quite different from each other, and practised their faith in very different ways. The Gospels mention three: the Scribes, the Pharisees and the Sadducees.

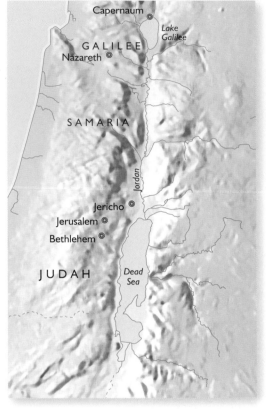

Palestine in the time of Jesus.

The **Scribes** were religious teachers, whose job was to explain the law of God to the people. In Matthew and Luke they are often linked with another group, the **Pharisees**, often shown as the main opponents of Jesus. In fact, Jesus was closer to the Pharisees in some things than he was to the other groups. For instance, both Jesus and the Pharisees believed that one day God would raise the dead and give eternal life to the righteous. Another group, the **Sadducees**, did not believe this. Nor, it seems, did they want a rebellion against Rome.

But many Jewish people did long to be free from Roman rule and hoped that one day God would give back to his people the kingdom that had been so glorious in King David's time. Some groups looked for a coming king who would defeat the Romans. Some looked for a figure who would descend from heaven and announce the 'day of the Lord'. Some looked for more than one figure. Such a figure was often called the 'anointed one'. In Hebrew that is *mashiah,* which in English is 'messiah'. The Greek word for 'anointed one' is *christos*, which in English is 'christ'. So many people looked for the coming of the Messiah, or the Christ, but there was no one view of what he would be like.

In the years before the Jewish War, an organized group called the **Zealots** emerged, planning armed resistance. There had been other outbreaks of violence against the Romans before that, and the word 'Zealot' may have been used to describe those who took part in them. In Luke and Acts it says that Simon, one of the followers of Jesus, was (or had been) a Zealot.

Josephus, the Jewish historian who took part in the Jewish War, describes another group, not mentioned in the Gospels, called the **Essenes**. These seem to have been close to the community at Qumran who wrote the Dead Sea Scrolls. Another group were the **Samaritans**, who lived in the area between Galilee and Judaea.

On the whole, the Romans did not interfere with the local religions of the empire. They wanted to keep the empire orderly and peaceful. But some Jews wanted the Romans out and were prepared to fight them. Other Jews wanted the Romans out, but were prepared to make the best of things. Others again believed that God would get rid of the Romans one day. Some, like the tax collectors, were glad to work for the Romans and get rich, even if it made them unpopular.

And then there was Jesus, who fitted into none of these groups.

The Samaritans

The Samaritans, or people of the region called Samaria, are mentioned in all the Gospels. While the Jews and the Samaritans were both descended from the twelve tribes of Israel, they regarded each other as foreigners. It seems that they usually avoided having anything to do with each other. Josephus says that the Samaritans were not allowed into the Temple at Jerusalem. Their own place of worship was on Mount Gerizim, and they accepted only the five 'books of Moses' (Genesis, Exodus, Leviticus, Numbers and Deuteronomy) as their holy books. Jesus welcomed and healed Samaritans, and one of his most famous stories (parables) is about the 'Good Samaritan' who stopped to help an injured Jew. The Samaritans have survived to the present day, faithful to their ancient religious practices. There are now only about 700 Samaritans, and they live either on Mount Gerizim, near the city of Nablus (Shechem in the Bible) or in Holon near Tel Aviv.

One of the jars in which the 'Dead Sea Scrolls' were found. Under the rim is the Hebrew word for 'Rome'.

38   The Jewish War

Look it Up

Jesus speaks of the destruction of the Temple:
Matthew 24; Mark 13; Luke 19:41–44; Luke 21:20–24

After the time of Jesus, the Romans became even more unpopular in Palestine. The Roman governors (or 'procurators'), such as Felix (who is mentioned in the Acts of the Apostles), were often cruel and corrupt. In 66 CE, the procurator Florus seized a huge amount of gold from the Temple. This caused a riot in Jerusalem, and the Romans had to withdraw to the coastal city of Caesarea. The revolt spread through Palestine, and in 67 the Roman general Vespasian was sent with an army to put it down. He recaptured most of Palestine, and prepared to attack Jerusalem, which was in the hands of the Jewish rebels. Then the emperor Nero died, and for two years there was uncertainty about who would succeed him. In 69 Vespasian himself was made emperor, and he left his son Titus to besiege Jerusalem in the spring of 70 CE.

Inside the city, different groups of Jewish rebels were fighting each other. This weakened the defence of the city, and made it easier for the Romans. Even so, it took them three months to capture Jerusalem. They burned the Temple and massacred the people of the city. Titus returned to Rome with the Jewish rebel leaders as prisoners. They took the great seven-branched candlestick (the 'menorah') and other sacred treasures from the Temple, and put them in the temple of the goddess of peace in Rome.

The Temple was gone, and the daily sacrifices came to an end. Jerusalem was ruined and could not be lived in. The leaders of the Jewish people were dead. It was the end of the Pharisees, the Sadducees and the Essenes. The Christian community of Jerusalem was scattered.

Matthew, Mark and Luke all say that Jesus spoke of the future destruction of the Temple. Luke says that he wept because he could see that the people of Jerusalem could not see where their safety lay. They thought that if they fought against the Romans, God would be sure to give them victory. But Jesus knew that if they were determined to follow a way of violence, it would lead to disaster.

Even the terrible war of 70 CE was not the end of the fighting. Another rebellion broke out in 132 CE. The Roman emperor Hadrian had decided to build a Roman city called Aelia Capitolina on the site of Jerusalem, with a temple of the Roman god Jupiter. This provoked the Jews to rebel again. Their leader was Simon bar Kocheba or Kosiba. Once again, Jewish fighters defended the city against a huge Roman army, and once again, the Romans captured it. Thousands of Jews

The last glimpse of the menorah. The seven-branched lampstand from the Temple in Jerusalem is carried in Titus's triumphal procession. The carving is on the Arch of Titus in Rome.

were killed, and thousands more sold into slavery. Hadrian went ahead with building Aelia Capitolina, and forbade the practice of the Jewish religion throughout Palestine. Jews continued to live in other parts of the Roman empire, but there was no further Jewish war against the Romans.

The Western (or 'Wailing') Wall in Jerusalem: all that remains of the outer wall of the Temple. It is the holiest place of prayer for Jews today.

Josephus

Much is known about the war of 66–70 CE because of a Jewish historian, usually called by his Roman name Flavius Josephus, who was born about 37 CE and died about 100 CE. In 66, he was put in command of the Jewish rebel forces in Galilee. He was captured, but saved from death by predicting that the Roman general Vespasian would become emperor. He was now distrusted by the Jewish rebels, and acted as an interpreter for the Roman general Titus. When the war was over, he wrote a long account of it, called *The Jewish War*, and another history book, *The Antiquities of the Jews*. He mentions Jesus, John the Baptist and James the brother of Jesus, though some of what he says about them may have been rewritten by later Christian writers.

Masada, near the Dead Sea. This was a stronghold occupied by hundreds of Zealots during the First Jewish War. Rather than surrender to the Romans, most of them committed suicide.

39 Jesus: a Figure from History

Look it Up

Luke's historical setting:
Luke 2:1–2; 3:1–2

Pontius Pilate:
*Matthew 27; Mark 15; Luke 13:1–5;
Luke 23; John 18–19; 1 Timothy 6:13*

How can the life of Jesus be dated?

Herod ('the Great') was governor of Galilee under the Romans. The Romans made him 'King of the Jews' in 40 BCE, and he was always loyal to them. He died in 4 BCE so Jesus must have been born before that date.

Luke says that Jesus began his work in the fifteenth year of the rule of the emperor Tiberias, 28–29 CE, and that he was 'about 30 years old'. If Jesus was born in or before 4 BCE and baptized in 28 CE, then he was about 32 when he began to preach.

Most of what is known about Jesus comes from the four Gospels. But there is also some evidence from both Roman and Jewish writers of the time. The Roman historian Suetonius (70–140 CE) describes a disturbance in the Jewish community in Rome during the reign of the emperor Claudius, stirred up by someone called 'Chrestos'. This probably refers to the Christians, and 'Chrestos' is a mistake for 'Christus' or Christ. Another Roman historian, Tacitus (about 55–120 CE) says that the Emperor Nero blamed the great fire of Rome in 66 CE on the Christians; and Tacitus goes on to explain that their founder had been put to death in Judaea by Pontius Pilate. Tacitus's friend and contemporary Pliny the Younger, who was the Roman governor of Bithynia, writing in the year 122 CE, describes to the emperor Trajan the case of the troublesome Christians in his province, who meet illegally for the worship of Christ, 'as to a god'.

Pontius Pilate was the prefect (or governor) of Judaea from 26 to 36 CE. In 1961, an inscription was discovered in the coastal town of Caesarea Maritima in which Pilate is mentioned.

An inscription discovered in 1961 at Caesarea Maritima on the Mediterranean coast. It mentions Pontius Pilate.

A gold coin showing the head of the emperor Tiberius.

'He [Jesus] travelled all over Galilee preaching in the synagogues' (Mark 1:39). The ruins of the synagogue at Gamla in Galilee.

The two Jewish historians Philo (20 BCE – 50 CE) and Josephus (37–100 CE) describe Pilate as a brutal man who had to be removed from his post by the emperor. There are also passages in Josephus which mention John the Baptist and Jesus, but scholars do not agree whether these passages were written by Josephus or were added later by Christian editors.

The Christian movement was therefore known to writers outside the Bible in the first century CE. The picture given of Jesus in the four Gospels also fits well into what is known of first-century Palestine. The four Gospels do not always agree (see chapter 44). But the Gospels do paint a historically accurate picture of the place and time in which Jesus lived. They could not do this if all the stories of Jesus had been invented long after he lived.

The other books of the New Testament do not give much more information about the life of Jesus, but they help to show what the first Christians believed about him. The final four chapters of this encyclopaedia will look at what the New Testament says about his **birth**, his **teaching**, his **crucifixion** and his **resurrection**.

'Jesus got into one of the boats – it belonged to Simon' (Luke 5:3).

The Lord Jesus Christ

Jesus is described in many ways in the New Testament. The commonest word is 'Christ' or 'Messiah' (see the panel in chapter 15).

Another title often used is 'the Lord', which is also used in the Old Testament for God.

Sometimes Jesus himself is called 'God' in the New Testament. At the beginning of John's Gospel, Jesus is described as the 'Word of God' and the author goes on to say, 'the Word was with God, and the Word was God.' At the end of John's Gospel, when the disciple Thomas meets the risen Jesus he addresses him as, 'My Lord and my God!'

Counting the years

Six centuries after the birth of Jesus, a Christian scholar called Dionysius Exiguus had the idea of counting the years from the birth of Jesus. Until then, the Romans counted the years from the traditional foundation of the city of Rome (753 before Christ – or BC). The years from the birth of Christ were counted forwards and are traditionally called AD – Anno Domini, the Latin for 'in the year of the Lord'. Since Herod died in what is now called 4 BC, and Jesus must have been born earlier than his death, Dionysius's calculations weren't quite right.

Nowadays, historians and archaeologists often call the years after the birth of Christ CE (the Common Era), and the years before Christ BCE (before the Common Era). But the numbering is still that of Dionysius Exiguus.

40 ⁂ The Followers of Jesus

Look it Up

The Twelve:
Matthew 10:1–4; Mark 3:13–19;
Luke 6:12–16; Acts 1:12–26

The women who followed Jesus:
Mark 15:40–41; Luke 8:1–3;
Luke 10:38–42

The women who followed Jesus

Jesus had many female disciples, some of whom travelled with him as he moved about the country. The best known of these is Mary Magdalene. In all four Gospels she is mentioned as seeing Jesus after his resurrection. Paul's letters show that women had leading positions in the churches that he founded as well as in the church at Rome.

All four Gospels describe how Jesus gathered round him a group of followers or 'disciples'. They went with him as he travelled about Palestine preaching and healing. He was followed by both men and women.

A special group among his followers were 'the Twelve'. Their names are given in Matthew, Mark, Luke and the Acts of the Apostles. Among the Twelve, three were the closest of all to Jesus: Simon Peter, and the two brothers James and John. The Twelve are called 'apostles' in Matthew, Luke and Acts, though not in Mark. The word 'apostle' is also used in the New Testament for others, such as Paul. The word apostle means one who is sent out: a messenger, a missionary.

Jesus called his apostles from many professions, including the much-hated tax collectors.

The Gospels say that other people were drawn to Jesus and were his friends and followers, though they did not all give up their homes and work to travel with him. They were sometimes able to welcome Jesus into their houses. The 'upper room' in Jerusalem where Jesus and his disciples had the Last Supper might have belonged to one of these followers.

The Acts of the Apostles tells how the group of Jesus' disciples began to grow in numbers. Those who followed Jesus called themselves 'the Way'. In Antioch, they were for the first time called 'Christians' (followers of the Christ). Local groups of Christians met together, and their meetings were called 'church', which means 'assembly' or 'gathering'. They prayed, fasted, sang hymns, read the scriptures (the Old Testament), and on the first day of the week they celebrated the Lord's Supper in which they broke bread and blessed the cup of wine as Jesus did at his Last Supper. When new people joined their communities, they were baptized. When Paul wrote a letter to one or another church, it would have been read aloud in this gathering.

Mary Magdalene playing a lute. A painting by an unknown artist of the early sixteenth century.

The Christians believed that Jesus had been raised from the dead. They also believed that one day he would appear in all the glory of God. Then the dead would be brought back to life, those who had followed Jesus would be united with him and the world would at last become the place of God's kingdom.

John the Baptist

John the Baptist (or 'baptizer') was a prophet and preacher who called the people of Israel to turn away from wrong. He baptized or 'dipped' them in the River Jordan as a sign of their new way of life. He baptized Jesus (see, for example, Mark 1:1–11) and encouraged his followers to become followers of Jesus. He spoke out against King Herod Antipas and was beheaded by him (Mark 6:14–29). According to Luke's Gospel, he was Jesus' cousin (Luke 1:5–80). Paul sometimes came across groups of John's followers in his travels (Acts 19:1–7). John is also mentioned by the Jewish historian Josephus.

Peter

John's Gospel says that Peter came from Bethsaida beside Lake Galilee, and was brought to Jesus by his brother Andrew. He had the common Jewish name 'Simon'. Jesus gave him a new name, *Cephas*, an Aramaic word meaning 'rock'. In Greek this is *Petros*, in English 'Peter'.

All four Gospels agree that Simon Peter was a fisherman. In Matthew, Mark and Luke, Jesus tells him to follow him and says that he will go fishing for others (meaning that he will bring them to Jesus).

In Matthew's Gospel, Jesus says to him, 'On this rock foundation I will build my church.' In Luke's Gospel, he is told: 'strengthen your brothers.' In John's Gospel, he is told by the risen Jesus to care for and feed his sheep (Jesus' followers). In the Acts of the Apostles, it is Peter who first begins to give the good news of the resurrection to the people of Jerusalem. So it is clear that he had a leading role among the disciples.

But Peter did not always behave like a rock. When Jesus was arrested, Peter denied three times that he knew Jesus; but Jesus later forgave him.

In John 21:18, Jesus says to Peter, 'When you were young, you used to get ready and go anywhere you wanted to; but when you are old, you will stretch out your hands and someone else will bind you and take you where you don't want to go.' The Gospel writer adds: 'In saying this, Jesus was indicating the way in which Peter would die and bring glory to God.' Peter was probably put to death during the persecution of Christians by the emperor Nero after the great fire of Rome in 64 CE. Nero blamed this on the Christians, and the Roman historian Tacitus describes the savage punishments given them, including crucifixion.

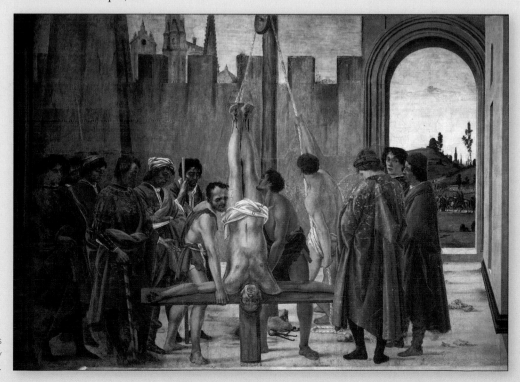

There is a tradition that Peter was crucified upside down. This painting is by Filippo Lippi (1457–1504) in Florence.

41 The Apostle Paul

How can the life of Paul be dated?

Acts 18:12–17 mentions Gallio as the procurator (or governor) of the Roman province of Achaia (part of what today is Greece). We know from an inscription discovered at Delphi that Gallio was procurator in 51–52 CE. This means that Paul was in Corinth in that year, on his way to Jerusalem. Paul says that three years after his conversion, he visited Jerusalem, and again fourteen years later. If that second visit to Jerusalem was in or about the year 52, then his conversion was in 33 CE, three or four years after Jesus was crucified.

The ruins of ancient Corinth. Paul's friends Priscilla and Aquila settled here after they had been forced to leave Rome by the emperor Claudius.

Paul is one of the most important figures in the New Testament. His letters are the earliest books of the New Testament to be written. He preached the Christian message in places where it had not been heard. He championed the revolutionary idea that Gentiles (people who are not Jews) could become Christians without having to accept all the laws of the Jewish religion. Although he was himself a Jew, he saw it as his special mission to bring Gentiles to know Jesus.

The Conversion of St Paul by Caravaggio (1571–1610), showing the moment when Paul was struck by light on the road to Damascus.

There are two ways of knowing about Paul's life: what he says in his own letters, and what Luke says in the Acts of the Apostles. From his own letters, it is clear that he was a Jew belonging to the tribe of Benjamin, and became a Pharisee. In the Acts, it is said that he came from Tarsus, a city of the Roman province of Cilicia (in modern Turkey), and was a Roman citizen. It is also said in Acts that his Jewish name was Saul; Paul (Paulus) was his Roman name. When the first followers of Jesus began to spread the Christian message, Paul says he became a 'persecutor of the church.'

Paul set out for the great city of Damascus to have the Christians there arrested and imprisoned. While he was on the way, he had a vision of Jesus and came to believe that Jesus was the Christ (the Messiah). He became a Christian himself, and began to preach the Christian message, travelling around the cities of the eastern Roman empire and setting up new churches (communities of Christians).

The Acts of the Apostles tells how many years later Paul was in Jerusalem to visit the Christian leaders there. There was a plot by some people who were opposed to the Christian message to get Paul arrested, and even murdered. He was indeed arrested by the Roman authorities, and he appealed to be tried in the emperor's court in Rome. So he was taken to Rome under arrest. In his letter to the Romans, he says he hoped to go to Spain, and perhaps eventually he did. There is no story of Paul's death in the New Testament, but there is the evidence of these words from 2 Timothy: 'As for me, the hour has come for me to be sacrificed; the time is here for me to leave this life. I have done my best in the race, I have run the full distance, and I have kept the faith. And now there is waiting for me the victory prize of being put right with God, which the Lord, the righteous Judge, will give me on that day.' These words suggest that Paul was put to death for his faith.

How did Paul die?

Paul's story in the New Testament finishes as he waits for trial in Rome. Thirty years later, Clement, a leader of the church in Rome, wrote to the church of Corinth about 'the noble figures of our own generation' who were 'persecuted and had to struggle even to death'. In particular, he mentions Peter 'who having borne his testimony went to his appointed place of glory', and Paul 'having borne his testimony before rulers, passed out of this world and went to the holy place'. The main persecution of Christians at the time of Paul's arrest and trial was that by the emperor Nero in Rome after the terrible fire of 64 CE. Traditionally, it is thought that Peter and Paul were both put to death in this persecution. Paul, as a Roman citizen, would have been killed with the sword. In Rome today you can see the great church of St Paul Outside the Walls, the traditional site of his burial.

The Basilica of St Paul Outside the Walls in Rome, the traditional site of Paul's burial. This church was completed in 1854 on the site of a church begun in the fourth century but destroyed by fire in 1823.

42 How Paul Wrote His Letters

Look it Up

One of Paul's best known messages – the meaning of love:

I Corinthians 13

'With my own hand I write this: Greetings from Paul' (Colossians 4:18). Paul would add a few words in his own handwriting to the letters that were written out for him.

Tychicus and Onesimus arrive in Colossae with a letter from Paul (Colossians 4:7).

Paul travelled from place to place, visiting churches (communities of Christians) or setting them up for the first time. He continued to care for the churches he started, and when he couldn't visit them himself, he wrote them letters (sometimes called 'epistles').

Probably the earliest to be written is his first letter to the Thessalonians (the people of the city of Thessalonica in what is today northern Greece). This makes it the first book of the New Testament to be written, in about the year 50, about twenty years after the crucifixion of Jesus.

Often Paul gives the names of those he was travelling with, as well as his own (see 1 Thessalonians 1:1: 'Paul, Silas [or Silvanus] and Timothy'). He often dictated his letters, and sometimes gives the name of the person who wrote it out for him. In Romans 16:22, his secretary adds, 'I, Tertius, the writer of this letter, send you Christian greetings.' Paul would then add something in his own handwriting; that was a way of making it clear that the letter really did come from him. At the end of Galatians, he says, perhaps as a joke, 'See what big letters I make as I write to you now with my own hand!'

A letter in the ancient world was an important way of keeping up a friendship between people who were a long way apart. When travel was uncertain, slow and dangerous, and people had none of the modern means of communication, the arrival of a letter was an exciting event. The whole Christian community would be gathered to listen to it being read aloud (Colossians 4:16). Paul's letters were no doubt carefully kept in each of the churches that received one. Later, they were collected together so that they could all be copied and passed from church to church. Even so, Colossians 4:16 mentions a letter to the church of the Laodiceans which has been lost.

Paul only wrote a letter when there was a need to do so. When he wrote to the Romans, it was to introduce himself to the Christian community in Rome before he went there.

When he wrote to the churches he himself started, he wrote to encourage them in their faith, and sometimes to warn them when he thought they were going wrong. Often it is possible to pick up from his letter what has been going on at that particular church. For example, in Corinth, some Christians had been saying that Jesus had not been raised from the dead, and were laughing at the idea. In 1 Corinthians 15, Paul sets out the reasons for believing that Jesus had indeed risen.

Modern readers often find it difficult to make sense of Paul. But people in his own time did as well. In the second letter of Peter, the writer says, 'Our dear brother Paul also wrote you with the wisdom that God gave him. He writes the same way in all his letters, speaking in them of these matters. His letters contain some things that are hard to understand…'

Did Paul write all his letters?

Paul usually had someone else to write out his letters for him. He often included the names of other people as well as his own at the head of his letters. A different choice of words, a different style, or what seems to be a different situation from Paul's own lifetime, have led some scholars to think that not all the letters come straight from Paul himself. The letters that have been questioned are 2 Thessalonians, Colossians, Ephesians, 1 and 2 Timothy, and Titus. The letter to the Hebrews, which does not have Paul's name in it at all, was also once thought to have been by him. It is possible that sometimes one of Paul's followers took things that Paul thought or said or wrote and enlarged his original letters. The writer may have been confident that he was continuing Paul's teaching, and humble enough not to put forward what he wrote in his own name.

The excellent network of Roman roads made it easier for Paul to travel around the empire. Some were well surfaced but in between towns they were much rougher. This is the Appian Way, by which Paul arrived in Rome (Acts 28:15).

43 🌴 Paul's Letters

Paul's letters are not printed in the New Testament in the order in which they were written, but roughly in order of length.

Paul's letter to the Romans
This is Paul's longest letter, written to the Christian church in the capital city of the empire. It was a church that had existed for years before Paul went there. Paul sets out a long argument to show what it means for both Jews and Gentiles to have faith in Jesus.

churches to which Paul wrote

Paul's first and second letters to the Corinthians
Corinth was an important centre of trade by land and sea in the province of Achaia (in what is now Greece). Paul wrote the first letter there at some point between 51 and 54 CE. It includes an account of the Last Supper, mentions those who saw Jesus after he had risen from the dead, and has a famous passage on the meaning of love. In the second letter, he describes his own experiences, including being beaten and shipwrecked.

The Forum, centre of ancient Rome.

Paul's letter to the Galatians
Galatia was a province of Roman Asia (in modern Turkey), and Paul's letter was addressed to all the churches in the different cities of the province.

Paul gives more information about his early years as a Christian, and an important statement about how Gentiles can become Christians without having to be converts to Judaism first. He probably wrote it at about the same time as Romans.

Paul's letter to the Ephesians

Ephesus was a city in the Roman province of Asia. Paul's preaching caused trouble, especially with the silversmiths of the city who made silver statues of the goddess Artemis. However, the earliest manuscripts of what we call 'the letter to the Ephesians' do not actually mention Ephesus. Some scholars think it is not by Paul and reflects the concerns of a later time. It speaks of the reconciliation of Jews and Gentiles, and indeed how the whole universe comes together in Jesus.

Paul's letter to the Philippians

Paul was very fond of the Christian community at Philippi, which he started in about 50 CE, his first foundation in what we would now call the continent of Europe. He wrote his letter from imprisonment, probably in Rome in the early 60s. He gives more information about his own life, saying for instance that he belonged to the tribe of Benjamin.

Paul's letter to the Colossians

Paul's companion Epaphroditus (or Epaphras) had preached the Christian message at Colossae, a city of the Lycus valley in the Roman province of Asia. As in other letters of Paul, this letter deals with the question of whether Gentile Christians should obey all the religious rules of the Old Testament.

The theatre at Ephesus. This is where the citizens of Ephesus met to protest about Paul's preaching (Acts 19:21–41).

Paul's letters to the Thessalonians

Thessalonica is a city in what is now northern Greece. Acts 17 tells how Paul and Silas arrived there from Philippi. They then moved on to Corinth, where it is thought that Paul wrote his first letter to the Thessalonians. This means that it is almost certainly the earliest of Paul's letters to have survived, and so the earliest piece of Christian writing. One of the matters Paul writes about is what happens to Christians when they die. The second letter speaks about the coming of Jesus.

Paul's letters to Timothy and Titus

These three short letters are sometimes called 'the Pastoral Letters'. The author writes about the organization of churches. Many scholars think that they come from the time after Paul, when questions of church organization might have become more important. Timothy and Titus were both companions of Paul whom he mentions in other letters.

Paul's letter to Philemon

This is Paul's shortest and most personal letter, written from one of his imprisonments to a Christian friend called Philemon about one of Philemon's slaves. The slave is called Onesimus, which means 'useful'. Onesimus had been with Paul, and had indeed been 'useful' to him. It may be that Onesimus had run away. In any case, while Onesimus was with Paul, Onesimus had become a Christian. So Paul writes to Philemon to ask him to welcome Onesimus back not just as a slave, but as a 'dear brother'.

44 How the Gospels Were Written

Look it Up

The three Synoptic accounts of the call of the first disciples:
Matthew 4:18–22; Mark 1:16–20; Luke 5:1–11

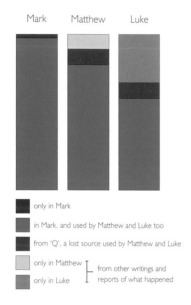

Mark Matthew Luke

■ only in Mark

■ in Mark, and used by Matthew and Luke too

■ from 'Q', a lost source used by Matthew and Luke

□ only in Matthew ⎤ from other writings and

■ only in Luke ⎦ reports of what happened

The above graph represents the relative amounts of overlap material in the Gospels of Mark, Matthew and Luke.

Before the Gospels were written down, Christians were telling each other what was remembered about Jesus. Paul says that when he became a Christian, he was told about Jesus' Last Supper, death, burial and resurrection. Other stories about what Jesus said and did were also handed on. We don't know when these remembered stories were first written down, but most scholars think that it began just before or after the fall of Jerusalem in 70 CE.

Two of the Gospel writers (or 'evangelists') explain why they wrote their Gospels. Luke, who addressed his book to someone called Theophilus, says that he wanted him to 'know the full truth about everything' that they had been told. John wanted his readers to 'believe that Jesus is the Messiah, the Son of God' and that 'through your faith in him you may have life.' Luke says that 'many people' had also written the story of Jesus; and John says that if everything that Jesus did had been recorded, 'the whole world could not hold the books that would be written.'

One of the other accounts of the life of Jesus which Luke knew about was almost certainly Mark's Gospel. Sixty per cent of Mark's Gospel appears, in almost the same words, in Luke. Eighty per cent of Mark appears in Matthew. It looks as though both Matthew and Luke

knew Mark's Gospel, and then added more material from other sources. This is why most scholars think that Mark was the first Gospel to be written. The similarities of these three Gospels is such that they can be set out side by side and looked at together ('synoptically'). Scholars call these three the 'Synoptic' Gospels.

John is rather different. He has not used Mark's Gospel in the close way Matthew and Luke seem to have done. Many of the stories he tells of Jesus are different from those in the 'Synoptic' Gospels. But he is familiar with the broad outline of the life of Jesus, his teaching, his death and his resurrection.

Papias was a Christian born about 30 years after the time of Jesus who was bishop of Hierapolis in Asia Minor and died about 130 CE. In a book which is now lost, but which was quoted from by other early Christian writers, Papias says that Mark wrote down in his Gospel what he had been told by Peter, and that Matthew wrote down the 'sayings' of Jesus. Papias's evidence is uncertain, but it shows what was being said about the Gospels in the generation after they were written.

About 150 CE, a Christian called Tatian put all four Gospels together into a continuous book. It was called the *Diatessaron*. Although it was read for a while, it was at last agreed that since the Gospels had been written separately, that was how they should be read. So there are *four* accounts of Jesus, not one; and each of the four sheds a different light on him.

Q – a lost source of the life of Jesus?

Some material (mostly sayings of Jesus) appears in a similar form in Matthew and Luke, but not in Mark. Some scholars think that this comes from a lost source that both Matthew and Luke knew about. This has even been given a name ('Q' – for the German word *Quelle*, a source) but no book like Q has ever been discovered. Other scholars think that the same stories about Jesus were being passed on by word of mouth, and both Matthew and Luke picked them up independently. Papias says that Matthew made a collection of the 'sayings' of Jesus, which is not a very good description of Matthew's Gospel, which has much more than the sayings of Jesus in it. 'Q', on the other hand, could have been just such a collection – is it 'Q' that Papias had in mind?

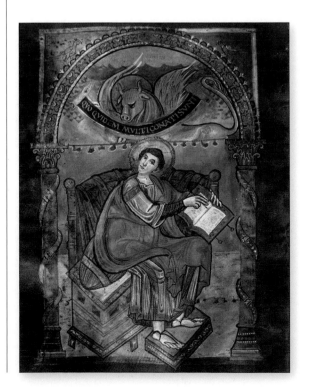

The Revelation of John speaks of four winged creatures that circle around the throne of God, looking like a man, a lion, an ox and an eagle. Since the fifth century, these have been thought to symbolize the four evangelists, Matthew, Mark, Luke and John. These pictures are from a book called the Gospels of St Riquier (the 'Charlemagne Gospels'), dating from about 800 CE.

45  Mark's Gospel

Look it Up

How did Mark begin his Gospel?
Mark 1:1–8

How did Mark end his Gospel?
Mark 16:1–8 or Mark 16:9–20

Mark's Gospel was almost certainly the first to be written. It is not clear who wrote it. Papias says that the Gospel was written by Mark from what was told him by Peter. But who was Mark? The Acts of the Apostles tell of 'John Mark', son of a woman called Mary in whose house in Jerusalem the first followers of Jesus used to meet. John Mark joined Paul and Barnabas in one of their preaching journeys, but after a while he left them and went home. Later Barnabas wanted to take John Mark with them again, but Paul refused. Paul however does mention Mark as one of his companions in several letters, and Mark is also mentioned in 1 Peter. But 'Mark' (*Marcus*) was a very common Roman name and it is not clear that all these Marks are the same person, or that any of them wrote what is called Mark's Gospel.

The writer (whoever it was) set out to write a book that would make people ask the question, 'Who is Jesus?' Throughout the Gospel, people ask questions about him. 'How does he dare to talk like this?' 'What wisdom is this that has been given him?' 'Why does he eat with such people?' 'What right have you to do these things?' 'What do you want with me?'

And Jesus also asks questions: 'What do you want me to do for you?' 'Why are you frightened? Have you still no faith?' 'Tell me, who do people say I am?' 'Who do you say I am?' Peter is the one who gives him the reply, 'You are the Messiah' (8:29). But then Jesus tells his disciples that the Messiah is not what they were expecting. 'The Son of Man must suffer much and be rejected by the elders, the chief priests, and the teachers of the Law. He will be put to death, but three days later he will rise to life.' The disciples find this hard to believe.

The rest of Mark's Gospel shows how this happened. Jesus provokes the anger of the authorities, who finally have him put to death. The one who healed the sick and cast out demons and spoke with God's authority and rode into Jerusalem as the Messiah is crucified.

'Jesus asked them, "Who do you say I am?" Peter answered, "You are the Messiah" ' (Mark 8:29).

94

Caesarea Philippi, formerly called Banyas after the Roman god Pan, who was worshipped here.
The niches in the rock are shrines dedicated to Pan. Here Peter acknowledged Jesus to be the Messiah.

Then comes one of the great puzzles of Mark's Gospel. Jesus has already promised his disciples that he would rise to life again, so we expect the story to finish with the resurrection. The body of Jesus is buried in the tomb. Some of his female followers come to visit it. They find it empty, and a strange figure (a 'young man') tells them that Jesus has risen. The women run away in terror.

That is where the earliest surviving manuscripts of Mark's Gospel stop. The risen Jesus does not appear. It is not clear if Mark meant his Gospel to finish at that point, or whether he left the book unfinished. This could be his way of putting one last question to the reader: 'And what do *you* think happened?'

Different endings of Mark's Gospel

Even if Mark meant to finish at 16:8, or if his original ending is lost, later manuscripts of the Gospel give different endings. In English versions of the Bible, these are either printed out as part of the main text or printed in a footnote. In one of these endings, Jesus tells his disciples to 'Go throughout the whole world and preach the gospel to the whole human race.'

46 Matthew's Gospel

Look it Up

The Sermon on the Mount:
Matthew 5–7

Matthew is called to follow Jesus:
Matthew 9:9

The Lord's Prayer

This prayer, also called the 'Our Father' (from its first two words), is from Matthew 6:9–13 and is often said in the following form:

Our Father in heaven,
hallowed be your name,
your kingdom come, your will
*   be done,*
on earth as [it is] in heaven.
Give us today our daily bread.
Forgive us our sins
as we forgive those who sin
*   against us.*
Lead us not into temptation,
but deliver us from evil.

An ancient ending is often added to the prayer:

For the kingdom, the power
and the glory are yours
now and for ever. Amen.

As with Mark's Gospel, it is not certain who wrote Matthew's Gospel. It is Papias who says that the evangelist was called Matthew. The Gospel mentions a tax collector whom Jesus called to follow him called Matthew (although in Mark and Luke he is called Levi), but that does not prove that this is the person who wrote the Gospel. After all, someone who had known Jesus so closely as Matthew the tax collector might not have needed to rely so much on Mark's Gospel. Matthew's Gospel was known to the Christian bishop at Antioch called Ignatius round about 100 CE, and most probably it was written in the years after the fall of Jerusalem in 70 CE.

This means that Matthew wrote at a time when the leaders of the Jewish religion (especially the Pharisees) were reorganizing themselves after the Jewish War. It was a time when Jewish people asked themselves what it meant to be Jewish. The Pharisees argued that it meant being faithful to the religion of their ancestors. They saw the Christian message as a betrayal of the Jewish faith.

Matthew wrote with a special concern for Jewish Christians. He wanted to show them that the Christian message was not the betrayal but rather the fulfilment of the Jewish faith. To be truly Jewish meant accepting Jesus as the Messiah. He emphasizes that Jesus himself kept the Law of Moses (5:17–20) and paid the Temple tax (17:24–27).

Matthew also emphasizes that the disciples of Jesus belong to a community – the church. 'For where two or three come together in my name,' says Jesus, 'I am there with them.' This was the time when Jewish Christians had to face the fact that they were no longer welcome in many of the synagogues – but they still had a community of their own.

The best known part of Matthew's Gospel is the 'Sermon on the Mount' (5–7) beginning with the 'Beatitudes'. Jesus here paints a picture of the people he calls 'blessed' (Latin *beati*): they hunger and thirst for justice, they are merciful, they are pure in heart, they are peacemakers. They are also 'poor in spirit', 'mourning', 'meek', and 'persecuted' – and these words will have meant a lot to those Jewish Christians who no longer felt welcome in the synagogues. But such people, says Jesus, are blessed by God and truly happy because they have reached 'the kingdom of heaven'.

The twentieth-century Church of the Beatitudes, marking the traditional site of the Sermon on the Mount.

'Go to the lost sheep of the people of Israel'

In Matthew 10:5, Jesus sends his disciples out on a preaching mission. It is very like Mark 6:7 and Luke 9:1. But in Matthew's version, Jesus goes out of his way to tell the disciples *not* to go to the 'Gentiles' (people who are not Jews) or to the Samaritans, but only 'to the lost sheep of the people of Israel.' Matthew suggests that Jesus' first aim was to call the people of Israel back to God. Only later on would he tell his followers to 'make disciples of all nations' (28:19).

The Beatitudes

'Blessed are poor in spirit,
for theirs is the kingdom of heaven.

'Blessed are those who mourn,
for they will be comforted.

'Blessed are the meek,
for they will inherit the earth.

'Blessed are those who hunger and
thirst for righteousness,
for they will be filled.

'Blessed are the merciful,
for they will be shown mercy.

'Blessed are the pure in heart,
for they will see God.

'Blessed are the peacemakers,
for they will be called sons of God.

'Blessed are those who are persecuted
because of righteousness,
for theirs is the kingdom of heaven.'

Matthew 5:3–10

47 Luke's Gospel

Look it Up

Luke, the companion of Paul:
*Colossians 4:14; Philemon 24 (verse);
2 Timothy 4:11*

This ancient building between Jerusalem and Jericho is known as the Inn of the Good Samaritan. It is the kind of building Jesus' listeners would have known.

The Vagabond. A painting of the prodigal son by Hieronymus Bosch (1450–1516).

Luke's Gospel has some of the best known of the stories about Jesus. Luke's version of the Christmas story is the one many people think of, with the angel Gabriel, the stable and the shepherds. Luke tells the only surviving story of Jesus as a boy. Only Luke's Gospel has the parables of the Good Samaritan and the Prodigal Son. Only Luke tells how Simon of Cyrene carried the cross of Jesus to his crucifixion. Only Luke says that Jesus forgave the soldiers who crucified him, and promised a place in paradise to the thief on the next cross. Only Luke tells the story of the two disciples who meet the risen Jesus on the road to Emmaus and take him to their home. Many of these stories highlight the generosity, hospitality, friendship and forgiveness that Jesus himself showed and encouraged in those around him. This is one of the special themes of Luke's book.

Who was Luke? As with the other Gospel writers, the author doesn't give himself a name. A Christian writer called Irenaeus who lived in what is now southern France in the second century CE is the first to say that the author was Luke. The only Luke mentioned in the New Testament was a doctor and a travelling companion of Paul. In Luke 1:2, the writer makes it clear that he does not claim to have known Jesus himself, but relies on those who 'saw these things from the beginning and who proclaimed the message.'

Luke's Gospel and the Acts of the Apostles are both dedicated to someone called Theophilus. This is one reason for thinking that both books come from the same writer.

At the time they were written, Christians were under suspicion from the Roman authorities. According to the Roman historian Tacitus, the emperor Nero had blamed them for the Great Fire of Rome. One of the reasons for writing both Luke's Gospel and the Acts of the Apostles was to show that Christians were not troublemakers in the way the Romans thought they were. For example, the way that Luke describes the trial of Jesus before Pontius Pilate shows that Pilate had no real reason to put him to death. In the same way, when Paul is put on trial before the Roman authorities in the Acts of the Apostles, the author shows how they have no case against him. So a main theme of both of Luke's books is that neither Jesus nor his followers were a threat to Rome.

'The twelve disciples went with him, and so did some women... Mary... Joanna... Susanna... and many other women' (Luke 8:1–3).

Who was Theophilus?

Both Luke's Gospel and the Acts of the Apostles are dedicated to 'the most excellent Theophilus' (Luke 1:3; Acts 1:1). The way he is addressed suggests he was a high-ranking official – maybe someone who could protect Paul while he was awaiting trial in Rome. But Theophilus clearly had a personal interest in Christianity in which he had already been 'taught' (Luke 1:4), so perhaps he was a new Christian and a friend of Luke's, who wanted Luke to write down all he knew of the Christian story.

48 The Acts of the Apostles

Look it Up

Stephen is stoned to death:
Acts 6:8–15; 7:54–60

Saul (Paul) is converted to Christianity on the road to Damascus:
Acts 9:1–30

James is killed by King Herod and Peter escapes from prison:
Acts 12:1–19

Paul and Silas are put in prison at Philippi and the prison guard becomes a Christian:
Acts 16:11–34

Paul is arrested in Jerusalem and then rescued from a plot to murder him:
Acts 21:27 – 23:35

Paul is shipwrecked on his way to Rome:
Acts 27:1–44

The book called the Acts of the Apostles tells how the first Christians took the message of Jesus out into the world. The action begins in Jerusalem, where according to the Gospels Jesus died and rose again. In the first part of the book the main characters are the apostles Peter and John, and two others among the first Christians called Philip and Stephen, who begin to take the Christian message to other places. The second part of the book tells how Paul became a Christian, and how he and his companions took the message still further – to Asia Minor and Greece, and finally as far as Rome. But although the book is called the Acts of the Apostles, nothing is said about what happened to any other apostle, except James, who was put to death.

The fact that both Luke's Gospel and the Acts of the Apostles are addressed to 'Theophilus' means that they are almost certainly by the same author. If that person really was Luke, the travelling companion mentioned in Paul's letters, then it might be expected that when the Acts reaches the account of Paul's travels, there might then be some evidence that the author was writing from his own experience. In fact, from Acts 16 onwards, the author begins to speak of 'we…'. He is also very detailed in his description of Paul's travels in the final chapters of the book, as if he has a very clear memory of those events. This is a strong reason for thinking that Paul's companion Luke really was the author. On the other hand, some scholars think that the picture he gives of Paul in the Acts is rather different from the picture that Paul gives of himself in his letters.

Paul used the excellent land and sea routes of the Mediterranean world to travel freely about the Roman empire.

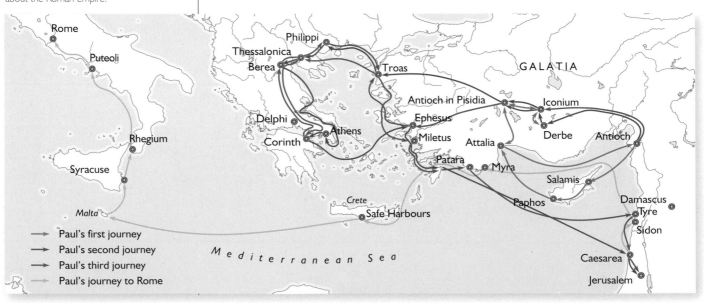

Paul's first journey
Paul's second journey
Paul's third journey
Paul's journey to Rome

The Acts of the Apostles describes not only how the young community of Jewish Christians began, but also how non-Jewish people ('Gentiles') became Christians as well. The author shows how Paul usually went first to the local Jewish synagogue, and then widened his message to Gentiles. In Athens, Paul addressed the Greek teachers of philosophy, quoting from a pagan poet to make his point. It is a main theme of the Acts that the good news of Jesus was for both Jewish and Gentile people.

The Acts come to an end with Paul awaiting trial in Rome. This could have been as far as the story had got (which would mean that the Acts were written in about 62 CE, with Luke's Gospel earlier, and Mark's Gospel even earlier than that). Alternatively, Luke might have planned a third book to tell the story of Paul's death. The most likely possibility is that he ended the story there because he had shown the Christian message being brought from the city of Jerusalem to the heart of the Roman empire.

Paul often travelled by ship. He says he was shipwrecked three times.

49 John's Gospel and Letters

Look it Up

What John says about his own writing:
John 20:30–31; 21:24–25; I John 1:1–4

The 'disciple whom Jesus loved':
John 13:21–30; 19:25–27; 20:1–10; John 21:20–23

People who might have known John

Irenaeus, bishop of Lyon in Gaul (France), lived from about 130 to 200 CE. He says in one of his books that as a boy he heard **Polycarp**, who was bishop of Smyrna in Asia Minor, and who lived from about 69 until he was put to death for his Christian faith in about 155. Irenaeus says that Polycarp 'spoke with many who had seen Christ' and that he knew John. This fits in with a tradition that John settled in Ephesus, about 50 kilometres from Smyrna. Irenaeus also mentions **Papias**, who was born about 60 CE and also became a bishop, and who had known both John and Polycarp.

John's Gospel records that Jesus said, 'I am the light of the world.'

John's Gospel goes to the heart of the Christian faith. This book sets out to say who Jesus is. He is the 'Word of God'. That is a way of saying that Jesus shows what God is really like. John's Gospel then goes on to say that the Word 'lived among us' (1:14). In Jesus, God was truly present, living a human life among human beings. At the end of John's Gospel, one of the disciples, Thomas, addresses Jesus as 'My Lord and my God!' (20:28).

The Gospel goes on to tell just how Jesus did 'live among us' – born, growing up, becoming hungry, being tired, relaxing with his friends, weeping, getting angry, attacking the powerful and proud, being put to death … and then rising again. In outline it is the same story that is found in the other three Gospels, though it also says things about Jesus that are not found there. Rather like Matthew's Gospel, the teaching of Jesus in John's Gospel is gathered into long speeches, but they are quite different from the speeches that Matthew gives, and quite different again from the parables that are found in all three 'Synoptic' Gospels.

Who wrote John's Gospel? The author was probably a Jew who knew the Holy Land well. The author doesn't name himself, but there is a figure in the Gospel called 'the disciple whom Jesus loved', by which perhaps the author means himself. Or perhaps he was someone able to pass on that disciple's story (see 19:35; 21:24). The 'disciple whom Jesus loved' lay next to him at the Last Supper (13:23), stood at the foot of the cross with Jesus' mother (19:26), went with Peter to visit the tomb of Jesus on Easter morning (20:2), and later walked with the risen Jesus on the lakeside (21:20).

From the second century CE, this figure has been taken to be the apostle John. So from that time, this Gospel has been called 'the Gospel according to John'.

The first 'letter of John' uses much of the same words and phrases as John's Gospel, and is almost certainly by the same writer. The second and third 'letters of John', which are much shorter, are from 'the Elder', who may be the same person as the author of the Gospel and the first letter, or may be someone else from the same Christian community. The letters all stress the importance of holding fast, as the first letter of John says, to 'the Word of life, which has existed from the very beginning. We have heard it, and we have seen it with our eyes; yes, we have seen it, and our hands have touched it.'

The light of the world

In John's Gospel, Jesus often describes himself in words that are quite different from those used in the other three Gospels. In Mark's Gospel, for instance, he often seems to want other people *not* to know who he was or what he was doing (for example, 5:43; 7:36; 8:30). It was not yet time for his message to be made too public. But John's Gospel is written with a different aim: to help everyone to see who Jesus is. Here are some of the things he says of himself in John's Gospel:

- I am the bread of life... Those who come to me will never be hungry (6:35).
- I am the light of the world. Whoever follows me will have the light of life and will never walk in darkness (8:12).
- I am the good shepherd, who is willing to die for the sheep (10:11).
- I am the resurrection and the life. Those who believe in me will live, even though they die (11:25).

The mother of Jesus and 'the disciple whom Jesus loved' gather at the foot of the cross, as told in John's Gospel. A thirteenth-century wood carving from Spain.

The John Rylands fragment

The earliest known manuscript of the New Testament in existence is a fragment of John's Gospel, discovered in Egypt in the early twentieth century and now on show in the John Rylands Library in Manchester, England.

It is dated to the early second century CE, perhaps only 30 or 40 years after the Gospel was written. It is from chapter 18: on one side verses 31–33 and on the other verses 37–38.

In the beginning the Word already existed; the Word was with God, and the Word was God. From the very beginning the Word was with God. Through him God made all things; not one thing in all creation was made without him. The Word was the source of life, and this life brought light to humanity. The light shines in the darkness, and the darkness has never put it out.

John 1:1–5

50 John's Revelation

The book that comes last in the New Testament is the Apocalypse or Revelation of John. ('Apocalypse' is from a Greek word which means the same as 'Revelation'.)

John says that he was in exile on the Greek island of Patmos (1:9) 'because I had proclaimed God's word.' This probably means that he was being punished for preaching the Christian message. In the first part of his book are letters to seven Christian communities in the Roman province of Asia (modern Turkey), including Ephesus.

An ancient church on the traditional site of John's Revelation on the island of Patmos.

This John has traditionally been taken to be the person who wrote John's Gospel and letters. Some people think that the style of the Revelation is so different from those books that it cannot come from the same writer. But this is a very different book from the Gospel and the letters, so that may account for the different style. It takes the form of a series of visions or revelations of what is going on in heaven. 'At this point I had another vision and saw an open door in heaven. And the voice that sounded like a trumpet, which I had heard speaking to me before, said, "Come up here, and I will show you what must happen after this."'

The book of Revelation describes an epic struggle between the forces of good and evil. In it, Michael the archangel defeats a dragon who is symbolic of the devil. This illustration is from a twelfth-century manuscript in the Bibliothèque Nationale in Paris, France.

In John's visions there are many echoes of the Old Testament, especially the books of Daniel, Ezekiel and Zechariah. There are descriptions of bloody cosmic battles at the end of time. (The words 'apocalypse' and 'apocalyptic' are often used to mean anything to do with the end of the world.) But John's main point is not to describe the end of the world, but to encourage Christians to stand firm in the face of persecution that was coming 'very soon' (1:1). However powerful the enemy may seem, he says, the victory has *already* been won by Jesus (5:5). In every period, Christians have found in John's Revelation a message of encouragement to live the Christian life in the face of persecution and difficulty.

The book ends with a description of the city of God set up in the middle of an earth that has been made new: 'I saw a new heaven and a new earth… And I saw the Holy City, the new Jerusalem, coming down out of heaven from God… I heard a loud voice speaking from the throne: "Now God's home is with human beings! He will live with them, and they shall be his people… There will be no more death, no more grief or crying or pain. The old things have disappeared"' (21:1–4). There are reminders of the Garden of Eden in the book of Genesis, as well as of Ezekiel's vision. Here flows the river of the water of life; here are trees whose leaves 'are for the healing of the nations'; here the servants of God 'will see his [God's] face'. They 'will not need lamps or sunlight, because the Lord God will be their light.' These are words that have both comforted and encouraged Christians at times of persecution, bereavement, darkness and death.

The Seven Churches of Revelation: the seven early centres of Christianity, as mentioned in the book of Revelation.

Heaven

'Heaven' is another word for the sky. In the Bible, 'heaven' (or the sky) stands for God's home, even though people knew that God could not be fitted into any space. As Solomon said at the dedication of the Temple, 'Not even all heaven is large enough to hold you' (1 Kings 8:27). In the earlier Old Testament period, people thought that when they died they lived on only in a sad place called Sheol, which meant 'the grave'. By the end of the Old Testament period, people were beginning to believe that at the end of the world, the dead would be brought back to life on earth, some to be punished and others to be rewarded (Daniel 12:2–3). This was called 'the resurrection', and in New Testament times, different Jewish groups still debated it. The Pharisees believed in the resurrection, but the Sadducees did not. Christians believed that Jesus had been raised from the dead as a sort of 'first instalment' of the resurrection of everybody. They spoke of those who died as 'asleep', waiting for the resurrection on the last day.

Later on, Christians began to have the idea that they would 'go to heaven' when they died, and that they would meet Peter at the gate of heaven, but this is not the way the Bible speaks of it.

51 The Last Letters

Therefore, since we are surrounded by such a great cloud of witnesses, let us throw off everything that hinders and the sin that so easily entangles, and let us run with perseverance the race marked out for us. Let us fix our eyes on Jesus, the author and perfector of our faith, who for the joy set before him endured the cross, scorning its shame, and sat down at the right hand of the throne of God.

Hebrews 12:1–2

Sixth-century mosaic of the saints in the Church of St Apollinare Nuovo in Ravenna. Standing inside the church, the visitor has a sense of being 'surrounded by the cloud of witnesses' described in the letter to the Hebrews.

The letter to the Hebrews

This long letter towards the end of the New Testament is something of a mystery. No name is given in the text of the letter either to the person who wrote it, or who it was sent to. Someone called Timothy and some people 'from Italy' are mentioned at the end, but these clues are not enough to explain more about it. The earliest manuscripts that have survived call it the letter 'to the Hebrews', but it is not clear that that is how the author addressed it. The mention of 'Timothy' gave some people the idea that it was written by Paul, and in some translations of the Bible it is called his letter, but the style of writing and the ideas are very different from anything we know to have been written by Paul. The letter is first mentioned by Clement of Rome, which means it must have been written by the end of the first century CE.

The letter to the Hebrews speaks of Jesus as the 'great high priest'. The high priest of the people of Israel would go into the Holy of Holies in the Temple once a year, carrying the blood of the animals killed in sacrifice in order to obtain forgiveness for the sins of the people. But, says the letter to the Hebrews, Jesus the true high priest has gone into the true Temple, which is God's dwelling in heaven. He has taken not the sacrificial blood of animals but his own blood, shed on the cross. He has gone there not once a year, but once for all, to bring forgiveness for all people.

This was what all the prophets of the Old Testament looked forward to, but never saw for themselves. In one passage, the writer recalls many of the heroes of the Old Testament – Noah and Abraham, Isaac and Jacob, Joseph and Moses, Gideon and Samson, David and Samuel and the prophets – those who 'fought whole countries and won… shut the mouths of lions… were mocked and whipped… stoned… The world was not good enough for them!' None of these, faithful as they were, says the writer, received what God was really promising, which only came true in Jesus. 'Therefore, since we are surrounded by such a great cloud of witnesses…' says the writer, 'let us run with perseverance the race marked out for us. Let us fix our eyes on Jesus' (12:1–2).

The letter of James

The letter of James (traditionally taken to be James, the brother of Jesus) is a favourite with many Christians because of its sturdy practical approach to living as a Christian. 'What God the Father considers to be pure and genuine religion is this,' he says:

'to take care of orphans and widows in their suffering and to keep oneself from being corrupted by the world.' There is an echo here of such Old Testament prophets as Amos and Jeremiah. The letter also urges people to treat poor people with as much respect as the rich: 'Suppose a rich man wearing a gold ring and fine clothes comes to your meeting, and a poor man in ragged clothes also comes. If you show more respect to the well-dressed man and say to him, "Have this best seat here," but say to the poor man, "Stand over there, or sit here on the floor by my feet," then you are guilty of creating distinctions among yourselves and of making judgments based on evil motives' (2:2–4).

The letters of Peter and Jude

One of the difficulties of thinking that 1 Peter was directly written by the apostle Peter is that it is written in the Greek of a very educated person, but Peter is spoken of in other parts of the New Testament as poorly educated ('Peter and John… were ordinary men of no education' – Acts 4:13). As in the case of some of the letters said to be by Paul, this may be a letter by someone else writing in Peter's name. It is a strong encouragement to Christians to stand firm in the face of persecution.

2 Peter is very different in style from 1 Peter, so it is hard to think both letters were by the same writer. It overlaps a lot with the letter of Jude, and both letters are a call to stand firm against false teachers in the church.

'Have this best seat here…'
'… sit here on the floor by my feet'
(James 2:3).

52 Collecting the Books of the New Testament

Look it Up

A young Christian brought up to read the (Old Testament) Scriptures:
2 Timothy 3:10–17

Paul's letters begin to be collected:
Colossians 4:16–17

Collecting the books of the Old Testament:
Chapter 32

An early attempt to cut down the Bible

In the middle of the second century CE there was a Christian in Rome called Marcion. He thought that the Old Testament and the New Testament belonged to two quite different religions, with different gods. He rejected the Old Testament, and felt there was too much influence of the Old Testament in the Gospels. He thought that Christians should only read the letters of Paul and an edited version of Luke. The church in Rome decided that Marcion was wrong, so he organized his followers into separate churches which lasted to the third century CE. But it was challenges such as this that made Christians think more clearly about which books they accepted and which they didn't.

For a whole generation, the first followers of Jesus preached his message, lived in his way and worshipped him, before any Christian books had appeared. They had the Old Testament, especially in its larger Greek form called the Septuagint. They had their memories of what Jesus said and did. There was also lively debate among Christian leaders about the right way to understand the teaching of Jesus, but they didn't have what is now called 'the Bible' to refer to. And when the books of what became the New Testament began to be written, they appeared in different churches and were not passed round all at once. No Christian could have seen *all* the books of the New Testament before the end of the first century CE.

But not even then, and not for a long time after that, were the 27 books of the New Testament regarded as a special collection on their own. Not all of them were accepted in all the Christian communities, and in many Christian communities other Christian books were read alongside them. It was another 100 years before most Christian

communities accepted most of the books now called 'the New Testament'. The first real list (called the 'Muratorian Canon') from about 200 CE has all the New Testament books except Hebrews, James, 1 and 2 Peter, but adds the 'Wisdom of Solomon'. The exact list (called the Canon) of the present 27 appears for the first time in a letter by Athanasius, bishop of Alexandria, in the year 367. That's more than 300 years since the first New Testament book was written.

Some of the other early Christian books are very close in their ideas to the books of the New Testament.

This fresco depicts Athanasius, the fourth-century bishop of Alexandria in Egypt, who wrote the letter in which the list of the present 27 New Testament books appeared for the first time.

For example, the first letter of Clement (written at the end of the first century CE) was read out in churches in the second century in just the same way as the letters of the New Testament. Another early Christian book is the Gospel of Thomas. Parts of this were discovered between 1898 and 1903, but most of it was only discovered in 1945. It was probably written in the middle of the second century CE, so cannot have been written by the Thomas who was one of the twelve apostles. It might just have some actual sayings of Jesus that are not found in the four 'canonical' Gospels, but they are mixed up with other ideas that were common in the second century CE. For instance, one idea in 'Thomas' is that women can only enter the kingdom of God by becoming men. This hardly fits the picture of Jesus in the four 'canonical' Gospels where he is exceptionally welcoming to women. Although 'Thomas' may have had a wide circulation among some Christian groups in the second and third centuries, it was not accepted into the Canon of the New Testament, and eventually it disappeared.

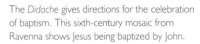

The *Didache* gives directions for the celebration of baptism. This sixth-century mosaic from Ravenna shows Jesus being baptized by John.

The *Didache*

A lost book called the 'Teaching of the Twelve Apostles' or the *Didache* (the Greek word for 'teaching') was quoted by many early Christian writers. The book was lost for centuries, but a copy was discovered in a monastery in Constantinople in 1873. Most scholars think that it was written in Syria in the early second century, though parts of it may be even earlier. It gives a vivid picture of the life of an early Christian community, with instructions about fasting, the Lord's Prayer, baptism and the Eucharist. It is quite close in its words and ideas to Matthew's Gospel. The *Didache* is another book that could easily have been included in the Canon of the New Testament.

A fragment of the Gospel of Thomas, discovered at Nag Hammadi in Egypt in 1945.

53 Jesus' Birth in the New Testament

Look it Up

Matthew's story of the birth of Jesus:
Matthew 1:18 – 2:23

Luke's story of the birth of Jesus:
Luke 2

The Blessed Virgin Mary

Matthew and Luke say that Mary was a virgin when she conceived Jesus. In Matthew, the angel says to Joseph, 'It is by the Holy Spirit that she has conceived.' In Luke, the angel says to Mary, 'The Holy Spirit will come on you, and God's power will rest upon you. For this reason the holy child will be called the Son of God.'

For Luke, Mary is the first to hear and receive the good news and that makes her the first disciple. A woman in the crowd listening to Jesus once said to him, 'Blessed is the mother who gave you birth and nursed you.' Jesus replied, 'Blessed rather are those who hear the word of God and obey it.' Mary was 'blessed' on both counts. She bore and nursed the Son of God, and she also heard and obeyed the word of God.

In the Song of Mary in Luke 1:46–55 (often called 'The Magnificat'), Mary says that 'from now on all generations will call me blessed.' So many Christians call her the Blessed Virgin Mary.

The Adoration of the Magi by Diego Velasquez (1599–1660) showing the wise men visiting the child Jesus, from Matthew's Gospel.

Matthew and Luke begin the story of Jesus before he was born, while Mark and John begin at the preaching of John the Baptist, when Jesus is grown up. Both Matthew's and Luke's stories are read in churches at Christmas. The Christmas story is so well known that it is hard to remember that Matthew's and Luke's versions are quite different from each other.

Luke describes how John the Baptist and Jesus were born, and how their births were announced by angels. He goes on to explain that Jesus was born in Bethlehem, although his mother Mary's home was in Nazareth. Mary and Joseph were in Bethlehem (which was where Joseph's family came from) because the Roman government was carrying out a census. There was no room for Mary and Joseph to stay in the inn, so they made do with the stable. There they were visited by shepherds. After going to the Temple in Jerusalem, Mary and Joseph returned home to Nazareth.

Matthew, on the other hand, mentions neither the census and the journey from Nazareth, nor the stable and the shepherds. After Jesus is born, he is visited in a 'house' in Bethlehem by wise men who have come from the east, bearing gifts. Then King Herod tries to have him killed, so Mary and Joseph escape with the child to Egypt. After that, when it is still not safe to go back to Judaea (where Bethlehem is) they go instead to Nazareth in Galilee.

The route from Nazareth to Bethlehem in Luke's story of the birth of Jesus, and the route from Bethlehem to Egypt in Matthew's story.

Those are some of the differences. Where do Matthew and Luke agree? Both say that Mary was a virgin at the time of her birth. Both say that Mary became married to Joseph. They agree that Jesus was born in Bethlehem and brought up in Nazareth. And they agree that Mary and Joseph were faithful and obedient to God, ready to do what was asked of them.

Neither Mark nor John describe the birth of Jesus, though the first chapter of John speaks of Jesus as the 'Word' of God coming into the world, becoming a human being and living among us. This is a passage read at many Christmas services.

In John's Gospel, people speak of Jesus as 'the son of Joseph', and it is nowhere said that Jesus was born in Bethlehem. There is even an argument (John 7:40–44) about whether Jesus could be the Messiah, because some people expect the Messiah to come from Bethlehem, while it was known that Jesus came from Nazareth in Galilee.

The other New Testament writers do not talk about the birth of Jesus, or mention Mary and Joseph, or speak about Jesus being born to a woman who was a virgin.

The Visitation by a follower of the thirteenth-century artist Giotto, showing Mary the mother of Jesus visiting Elizabeth the mother of John the Baptist, from Luke's Gospel.

Some Christmas stories not in the Bible

The wise men in Matthew's Gospel are often called 'kings' and pictured riding on camels. That picture was probably suggested by Isaiah 60:3–6 and Psalm 72:10–11. Their traditional names – Caspar, Melchior and Balthasar – are first mentioned in the sixth century CE. Luke doesn't say that Jesus was born in a cave, as can be seen in many old pictures; that comes from the *Protevangelium of James*, written about 150 CE. The same book gives the names Joachim and Anna (St Anne) to the parents of Mary.

Herod the Great

Herod ('the Great') was governor of Galilee under the Romans. His wife Mariamne was from the Hasmonaean family. The Romans made Herod 'King of the Jews' in 40 BCE, and he was always loyal to them. He was a harsh ruler, and would put up with no opposition, even having his own wife and sons killed. He planned the fine new port of Caesarea. His most famous building was the new Temple in Jerusalem, which he started in 20 BCE and was not finished until 62 CE. He died in 4 BCE, so Jesus must have been born before that date (see chapter 39).

The aqueduct built by Herod the Great to bring water into his new city of Caesarea.

Jesus said that the kingdom of God was like a big tree, with room for many birds to make nests in its branches (Luke 13:18–19). His words echo those of Ezekiel (17:22–24).

People called Jesus 'Teacher'. The Gospels say that people were astonished that he spoke with such knowledge and authority. But John's Gospel also says that when Jesus said things that were too difficult to understand, people stopped following him. He asked his twelve disciples whether they too would go away. Peter replied, 'Lord, to whom would we go? You have the words that give eternal life. And now we believe and know that you are the Holy One who has come from God.' That was the impact which Jesus made on them.

Jesus taught people by telling stories (often called 'parables'). Some of these are quite long, with several scenes and characters, like the parable of the Good Samaritan and the parable of the Prodigal Son. Others are short, more like a snapshot, such as this one: 'The kingdom of heaven is like this. A man happens to find a treasure hidden in a field. He covers it up again, and is so happy that he goes and sells everything he has, and then goes back and buys that field.'

In Mark and Luke, Jesus speaks about the **kingdom of God**. In Matthew it is called the **kingdom of heaven**, but it means the same thing. Jesus says that the kingdom is 'near' (Mark 1:15). When a teacher of the Law says to Jesus that it is more important to love God and one's neighbour than to offer sacrifices, Jesus replies, 'You are not far from the kingdom of God' (Mark 12:34). In Matthew 5:3–12, Jesus paints a picture of the people of the kingdom: they hunger and thirst for justice, they are pure in heart, they are merciful, they are peacemakers. Jesus calls them 'blessed' – blessed by God and truly happy.

Jesus said that some surprising people could reach the kingdom. It wasn't just the religious leaders of the time, nor only the people of Israel. They could be Samaritans, Romans and Greeks. They would come 'from the east and the west and sit down with Abraham, Isaac, and Jacob at the feast in the kingdom of heaven.' They could include prostitutes and tax collectors – people whom no one expected in God's kingdom.

It was for saying such things that the religious leaders of the time were so angry with Jesus that they wanted to put a stop to him.

As well as telling stories, Jesus gave long talks or sermons. John recounts the teaching of Jesus in words that are different from those in the other Gospels (see chapter 44). But John also describes unexpected people coming to believe in him. For instance, it was difficult for Jewish people to think of Samaritans as part of God's kingdom. But just as Luke gives Jesus' story of the Good Samaritan, so in John there is an account of a Samaritan woman who came to believe that Jesus was the Messiah.

Jesus taught with actions as well as words. All the Gospel writers say that he healed the sick and cured those who were possessed by demons. Once, John the Baptist sent his own followers to find out whether Jesus really was the Messiah. Jesus simply replied, 'Go back and tell John what you are hearing and seeing: the blind can see, the lame can walk, those who suffer from dreaded skin diseases are made clean, the deaf hear, the dead are brought back to life, and the Good News is preached to the poor.'

Paul has much to say about Jesus, but he doesn't quote any of his words, except his words at the Last Supper, and one other saying which is not in any of the Gospels. Paul says: '… remembering the words that the Lord Jesus himself said, "There is more happiness in giving than receiving." '

'Do this in memory of me'

Matthew and Mark tell us that at the 'Last Supper', on the night before he died, Jesus took bread, gave thanks, broke it and gave it to his disciples saying, 'This is my body.' He blessed and gave them wine saying, 'This is my blood.' Luke gives a similar account, and adds that Jesus told his disciples: 'Do this in memory of me.' The first Christians regularly kept the same holy meal, as is clear from Paul's first letter to the Corinthians, where he describes the Last Supper in words very like those of Matthew, Mark and Luke (I Corinthians 10:16–17; 11:17–32). They called it 'the Lord's Supper' or the 'breaking of bread'. Christians have continued to keep the Lord's Supper, and in different churches it may be called 'the Eucharist', 'the Liturgy', 'the Mass' or 'Holy Communion'.

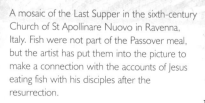

A mosaic of the Last Supper in the sixth-century Church of St Apollinare Nuovo in Ravenna, Italy. Fish were not part of the Passover meal, but the artist has put them into the picture to make a connection with the accounts of Jesus eating fish with his disciples after the resurrection.

Look it Up

The crucifixion:
Matthew 27; Mark 15; Luke 23; John 19

What Paul says about the crucifixion

The death of Jesus was very important to **Paul**, and is spoken about in almost all his letters. He speaks of Jesus as being 'humble' and walking 'the path of obedience all the way to death – his death on the cross.' He speaks of the 'rulers of this world' who 'crucified the Lord of glory.' For Paul, the death of Jesus is 'powerful' because it is God's way of reaching out to the whole world. 'God was reconciling the world to himself in Christ,' he says.

In John's account of the crucifixion, the soldiers threw dice to decide which of them would have Jesus' clothes. This was the right of Roman soldiers who took part in an execution.

The four Gospels agree that Jesus was crucified on the orders of the Roman governor Pontius Pilate during the Passover festival in Jerusalem. Although each Gospel writer tells the story in his own way, their accounts of Jesus' death agree more closely than in some other parts of the Gospels.

All four Gospel writers agree that the Jewish leaders were more and more angry at what Jesus was saying and doing. For Jesus to stay up north in Galilee was one thing; for him to come to Jerusalem and spread his teaching there was much more dangerous. In all four Gospels, Jesus rides into Jerusalem on a donkey, and is cheered by the pilgrims who have come to the city for the Passover. Nothing could have looked more plainly like the king foretold by the prophet Zechariah: 'Shout for joy, you people of Jerusalem! Look, your king is coming to you! He comes triumphant and victorious, but humble and riding on a donkey' (Zechariah 9:9).

Matthew, Mark and Luke also describe how Jesus took over the Temple. He cleared out the people who were using the Temple as a marketplace, and spent some days there healing the sick and teaching the people. (John says this happened during an earlier visit to Jerusalem – John 2:13–22.)

From then on, the Jewish authorities wanted Jesus done away with. They had to persuade Pontius Pilate that Jesus was dangerous; they also had to find a way of having Jesus killed without bringing the crowd out on his side. The four Gospels all say that Jesus was betrayed (Matthew and Mark call the place Gethsemane; John says it was a garden) by one of his disciples, Judas. The officers of the Temple guard arrested Jesus under cover of darkness. There followed a hasty trial before the high priest and the ruling council, where it was agreed that Jesus was guilty of blasphemy (speaking and acting against God).

Jesus was hurried to Pilate, where he was accused of claiming to be king of the Jews. All four Gospel writers say that Pilate could see no reason for Jesus to be punished, but to avoid a riot he still allowed him to be killed. So Jesus was crucified, one of the Romans' favourite ways of executing people. It was a cruelly slow and painful way to die. For a Jewish person to be crucified, there was something worse even than the pain. They had been taught that 'anyone who is hung on a tree is under God's curse' (Deuteronomy 21:23).

The way **Mark** and **Matthew** tell the story of the crucifixion is very bleak. Jesus says nothing on the cross except to shout out a verse from the psalms: 'My God, my God, why did you abandon me?' (see chapter 17). The priests who have had him condemned, the passers-by, and even the men being crucified alongside him all mock him. His only support comes from his women followers, who stand a long way off.

In **Luke**'s account, Jesus speaks more often. He asks God his Father to forgive the men who crucify him. To the thief on the next cross, he promises a place with him in 'paradise' (which here probably means a place of rest for righteous people after death). As Jesus dies, he uses another verse from the psalms: 'Father, into your hands I commit my spirit' (Psalm 31:5). He is more resigned, less anguished, than in Matthew and Mark.

John's Gospel always emphasizes that Jesus remains in control of the situation. Though he died, it was because he chose to 'give his life'. 'No one takes my life away from me,' he says. At the foot of the cross are the unnamed 'disciple whom Jesus loved' and his mother. Jesus speaks to them both, and tells them to care for each other. As he dies, he says, 'It is finished!' meaning that everything he had come into the world to do had now been done.

Other New Testament books

Other New Testament writers also have much to say about the death of Jesus. In the **letter to the Hebrews**, it is said that Jesus 'suffered death, so that… he might taste death for everyone.' Jesus 'made his prayers and requests with loud cries and tears to God' (which sounds like the story of Jesus in the Garden of Gethsemane). Jesus 'died outside the city,' meaning he was put outside the fellowship of God's people.

In the **Revelation of John**, Jesus appears as a 'lamb' (the animal of sacrifice) that 'appeared to have been killed.' Revelation also speaks of the city where the 'Lord was crucified.'

Ancient olive trees in what is traditionally regarded as the Garden of Gethsemane.

56 Jesus' Resurrection in the New Testament

Look it Up

The four Gospel writers tell the story of the resurrection in their own words:
Matthew 28; Mark 16; Luke 24; John 20–21

And Paul tells it in his:
1 Corinthians 15

A painting of the resurrection by Pietro Perugino (1446–1524) in the Convent of San Pietro, Perugia, Italy. The costumes and landscape are those of sixteenth-century Italy – the artist has imagined the resurrection of Jesus happening in his own situation.

The crucifixion could have been the end of anyone believing that Jesus was the Messiah. The grief and despair of Jesus' disciples is well expressed in Luke's story of two of them leaving Jerusalem after the crucifixion. 'We had hoped that he was the one who was going to redeem Israel,' they said. 'We had hoped' – but now it was all over.

The body of Jesus was quickly buried by his friends, as the following day was the sabbath when nothing was allowed to be done. Matthew says that Pilate allowed the chief priests to set soldiers to guard the tomb.

In different ways, all four Gospels tell of the female followers of Jesus going to the tomb early on the day after the sabbath. They all say that they found the tomb empty. **Mark, Matthew** and **Luke** tell of one or two figures in white who say that Jesus has risen. Mark says that the women were terrified and ran away, and that is where the earliest form of his Gospel ends.

In Matthew and Luke, the women go to tell the other disciples. Then Jesus himself begins to appear. In Matthew, Jesus says

116

the disciples are to go to Galilee, and there they meet him on a mountain top. In Luke, he says they are to remain in Jerusalem until they receive the gift of the Holy Spirit. Luke also tells of two disciples meeting Jesus on the road to the village of Emmaus. When they were in the disciples' house, Jesus 'broke the bread' at the beginning of supper, and it was at that moment that they recognized him.

John mentions no figures in white, but Jesus himself appears first to Mary Magdalene in the garden. Then he comes to the disciples that evening, and again a week later, and Thomas (who didn't at first believe) is convinced. Then John gives a further account of Jesus meeting the disciples beside Lake Galilee.

Paul, writing before any of the Gospels were written, tells the Corinthians what he himself had been told: that Jesus died and was buried, and that he was raised to life on the third day. He lists those who saw Jesus alive, including 'Cephas' (Peter), all twelve apostles, James and 'more than 500' disciples at one time, 'most of whom are still alive.' Then he goes on to speak of his own meeting with Jesus (when he saw him on the road to Damascus). Paul speaks about the resurrection in many other places. For him it was the way God showed that the crucifixion was not the defeat of Jesus. It was the beginning of a new age, and because of it all who believed in Jesus would in the end be raised to life.

The other New Testament writers also make much of the resurrection. Here is one example (1 Peter 1:3–4): 'Let us give thanks to the God and Father of our Lord Jesus Christ! Because of his great mercy he gave us new life by raising Jesus Christ from death. This fills us with a living hope, and so we look forward to possessing the rich blessings that God keeps for his people.'

In the fourth century, Helena, the mother of the emperor Constantine, built a church on the traditional site of the sepulchre where Jesus was buried. The present church dates mainly from the medieval period. This is the Chapel of the Angel, at the entrance of the Tomb of Christ in the Church of the Holy Sepulchre.

The tomb of Jesus

The Jews buried their dead. Rich people often had caves prepared for their burial with a ledge on which to lay the body. Sometimes there were large flat circular stones that could be rolled across the opening of the cave. This was the kind of tomb (or 'sepulchre') in which Jesus was buried after his death, quickly so that it could be done before the sabbath began (Matthew 27:57–66).

The tomb of Jesus has never been definitely identified, but the traditional place is what is now the Church of the Holy Sepulchre in Jerusalem.

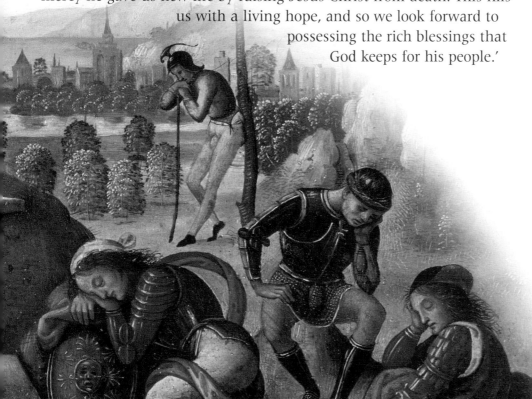

What people have said about the Bible:

All sacred scripture is but one book, and that one book is Christ, because all divine scripture speaks of Christ, and all divine scripture is fulfilled in Christ.

Hugh of St Victor (medieval French scholar, died 1142)

The Ten Commandments have helped to shape not only Judaism and Christianity, but the whole modern world.

At the beginning of *The Lion Encyclopedia of the Bible*, the Bible was described as being a book of stories – stories from the past to give hope for the future. Jews read the Hebrew Bible (the Torah) in this way, and Christians read the Christian Bible (the Old Testament and the New Testament) in this way.

Sometimes the 'hope' that the Bible has given has just been to carry on through difficult times. At other times, the Bible has spurred people to change the world. For example, the slaves in the United States in the nineteenth century sang songs based on Bible words called 'spirituals' to keep up their spirits even though their situation seemed hopeless. When slavery was made illegal in the British empire, it was due to a campaign of Christian people who believed that the Bible was against slavery. But they had to argue with other Christians who thought the Bible allowed it.

Martin Luther King, the great champion of civil rights for black Americans, was encouraged by what he read in the Bible. So was Dietrich Bonhoeffer, the brave German pastor who opposed Hitler during the Second World War. Both bravely carried their beliefs into action, and were killed for it – like John the Baptist, James, Stephen, Peter and Paul. But King and Bonhoeffer both had to argue with other Christians, who thought they got the Bible wrong.

The Bible inspired the protests of Christians against apartheid in South Africa, but other Christians argued that the Bible said that races should be kept separate. This shows that the Bible has been read in different ways by different people. Today, Christians disagree about what the Bible teaches about homosexuality, and many other issues. There are those who think the Bible gives too little place to women. Others emphasize how much the Bible speaks about women, but believe that Christians down the ages have not paid much attention to this.

The Bible has encouraged people who are neither Jews nor Christians. Mahatma Gandhi, a Hindu, who was the advocate of non-violent revolution and the maker of modern India, meditated deeply on Jesus' Sermon on the Mount.

For Christians, the main story of the Bible is the story of Jesus. The Old Testament prepares the way for him, and the New Testament tells about him. The whole Bible points to him. Christians remember that in John's Gospel, Jesus says: 'You study the Scriptures [the Bible], because you think that in them you will find eternal life. And these very Scriptures speak about me!' (John 5:39).

Jesus told his followers to feed the hungry, to clothe the naked, and to visit the sick and those in prison, and that when these things were done for others they were also done for him (Matthew 25:31–40). The relief organization Christian Aid has helped to build a dam to bring water to this village in Mali, Africa.

The city of Jerusalem is sacred to Jews, Christians and Muslims. Members of these three faiths consider themselves to be 'people of the book' because they share some of the same ancient stories.

Timeline

Dates in *italics* are approximate

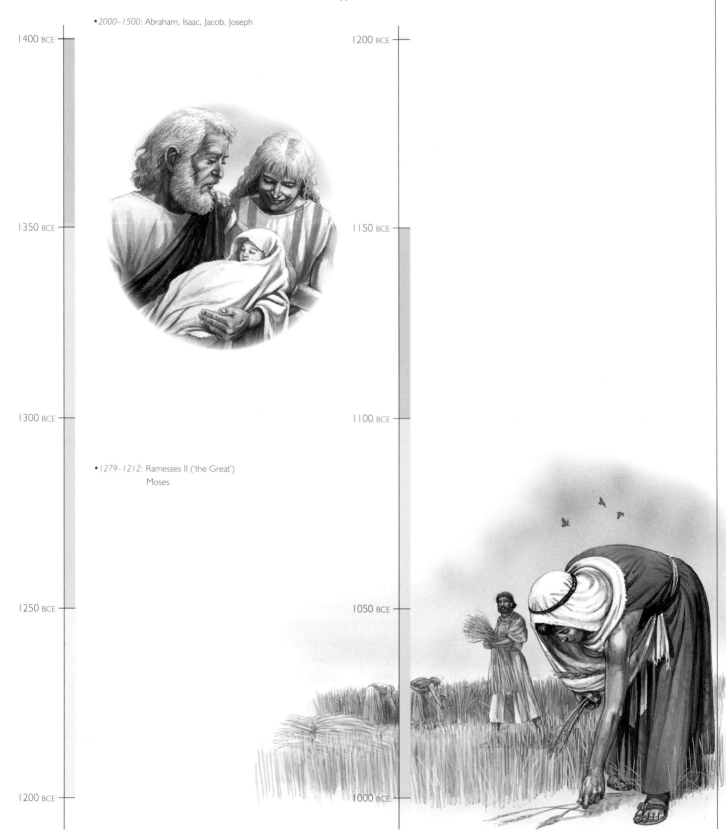

• *2000–1500*: Abraham, Isaac, Jacob, Joseph

1400 BCE

1350 BCE

1300 BCE

• *1279–1212*: Ramesses II ('the Great')
  Moses

1250 BCE

1200 BCE

1200 BCE

1150 BCE

1100 BCE

1050 BCE

1000 BCE

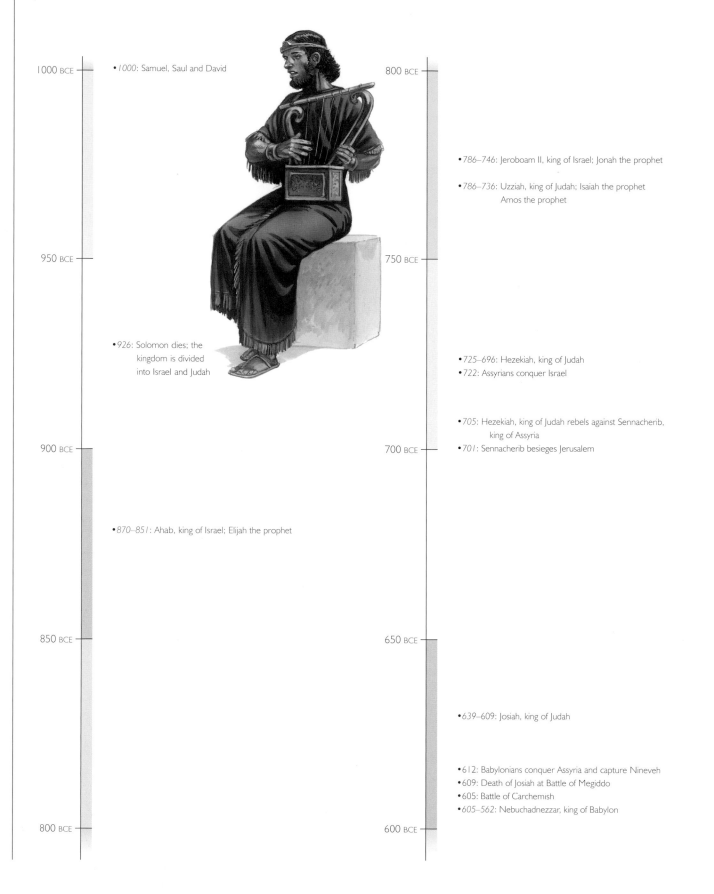

1000 BCE —

• *1000*: Samuel, Saul and David

950 BCE —

•*926*: Solomon dies; the
    kingdom is divided
    into Israel and Judah

900 BCE —

•*870–851*: Ahab, king of Israel; Elijah the prophet

850 BCE —

800 BCE —

800 BCE —

•*786–746*: Jeroboam II, king of Israel; Jonah the prophet

•*786–736*: Uzziah, king of Judah; Isaiah the prophet
    Amos the prophet

750 BCE —

•*725–696*: Hezekiah, king of Judah
•*722*: Assyrians conquer Israel

•*705*: Hezekiah, king of Judah rebels against Sennacherib,
    king of Assyria
•*701*: Sennacherib besieges Jerusalem

700 BCE —

650 BCE —

•*639–609*: Josiah, king of Judah

•*612*: Babylonians conquer Assyria and capture Nineveh
•*609*: Death of Josiah at Battle of Megiddo
•*605*: Battle of Carchemish
•*605–562*: Nebuchadnezzar, king of Babylon

600 BCE —

Timeline continued

Dates in *italics* are approximate

600 BCE

- *597*: Nebuchadnezzar invades Judah and captures Jerusalem
  Jeremiah the prophet
- *587/586*: Nebuchadnezzar destroys the Temple

550 BCE

- 539: Cyrus, king of Persia conquers Babylon and allows the Jews to return to Jerusalem

500 BCE

- 486–465: Xerxes I, king of Persia

450 BCE

400 BCE

400 BCE

350 BCE

- 334: Alexander the Great, king of Macedon invades Persian empire
- 323: Alexander the Great dies and his empire is divided

300 BCE

250 BCE

200 BCE

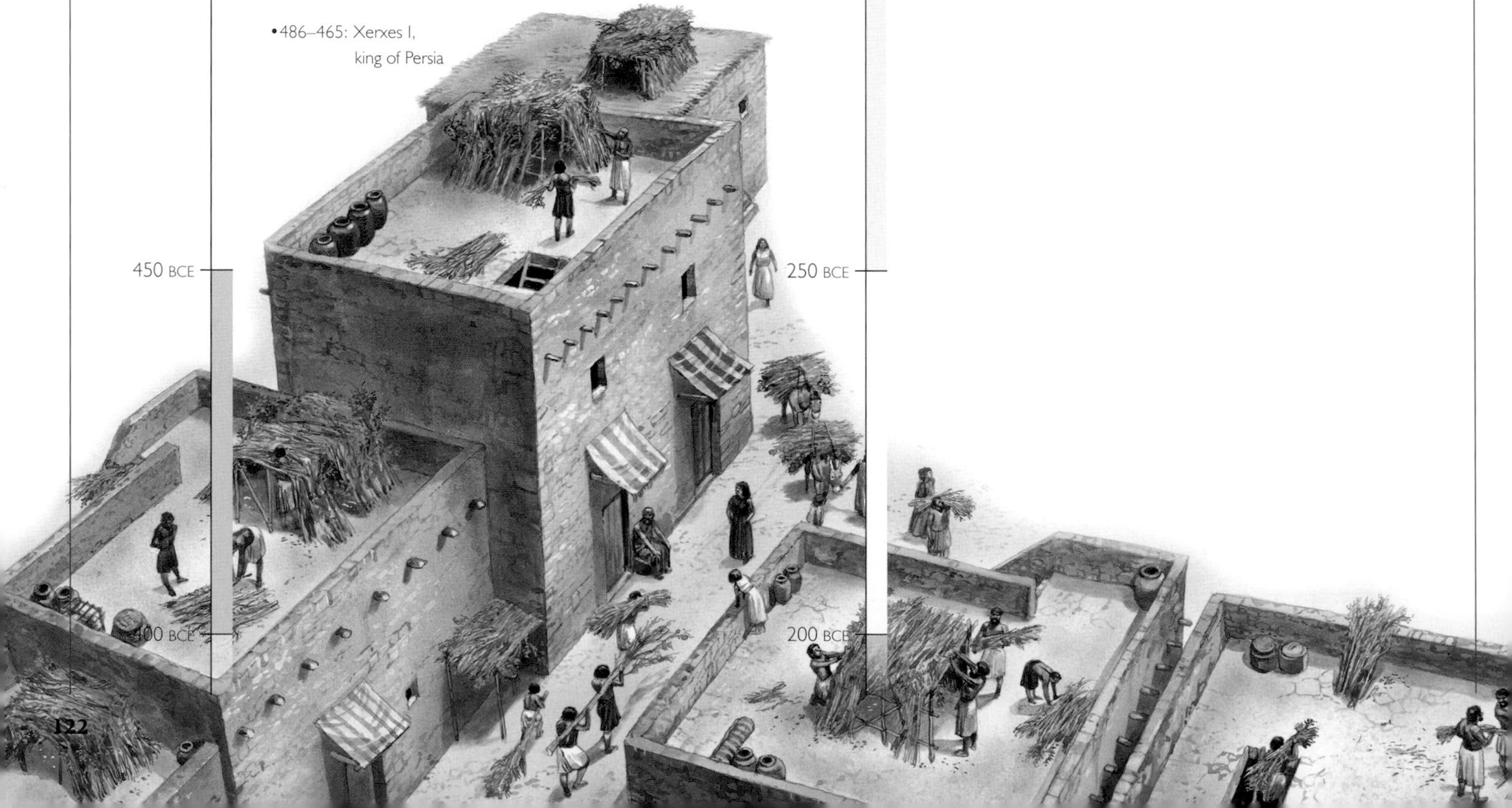

200 BCE

•167: Maccabean Revolt
•164: Rededication of the Temple
•161: Death of Judas Maccabaeus

150 BCE

100 BCE

•63: Pompey the Great conquers Palestine

50 BCE

•40: Herod the Great made 'king of the Jews' by the Romans

•27 BCE – 14 CE: Augustus reigns as emperor
•20: Herod the Great begins rebuilding of Temple

•4: Death of Herod the Great
•4: Jesus born

CE

CE

•14–37: Tiberius reigns as emperor

•26–36: Pontius Pilate, prefect of Judaea
•28: Jesus baptized
•29–30: Jesus crucified
•33: Paul converts to Christianity

•41–54: Claudius reigns as emperor

50 CE

•49: Claudius expels all Jews from Rome
•50: Paul writes 1 Thessalonians; begins church in Philippi
•51–52 Gallio, procurator of Achaia; Paul in Corinth
•54–68: Nero reigns as emperor
•60: Papias born
•62: Herod's Temple finished
•64: Great Fire of Rome followed by persecution of Christians
        (including, perhaps, the martyrdom of Peter and Paul)
•66: Jewish War
•69: Polycarp born
•70: Jerusalem captured by the Romans; the Temple destroyed
•73: Masada captured by the Romans; the end of the Jewish War
•81–96: Domitian reigns as emperor
•95: John's Revelation
•96: Clement's letter to the Corinthians
•90–100: The Didache

100 CE

150 CE

•130: Irenaeus is born; Papias dies
•144: Marcion excommunicated at Rome
•150: Gospel of Thomas
•150: Tatian's Diatessaron
•Second century: Protevangelium of James
•155: Martyrdom of Polycarp

200 CE

•200: Muratorian Canon; Irenaeus dies

Index